Building meaning in context:
A dynamic approach to Bantu clause structure

Publications of the Philological Society, 49

Building meaning in context:
A dynamic approach to Bantu clause structure

Hannah Gibson
University of Essex

Publications of the Philological Society, 49

WILEY
Blackwell

BUILDING MEANING IN CONTEXT: A DYNAMIC APPROACH TO BANTU CLAUSE STRUCTURE

Hannah Gibson

University of Essex

For my brother Richard. Open to grace.

ABBREVIATIONS

Glossing follows the Leipzig Glossing Rules. The following abbreviations are used:

1, 2, 3 etc.	noun class 1, 2, 3 etc.
1sg	first person singular etc.
2pl	second person plural etc.
ACC	accusative
APPL	applicative
AUG	augment
AUX	auxiliary
CAUS	causative
CJ	conjoint
CON	construct case
COND	conditional
CONN	conjunction
CONT	continuous
CNTREXPECT	counter-expectational
CONSC	consecutive
COP	copula
DEM	demonstrative
DET	determiner
DIM	diminutive
DIST	distal
DU	declarative unit
F	feminine
Fo	formula
FV	final vowel
FUT	future
FUT1	near future
GEN	genitive
HAB	habitual
IMP	imperative
IMPFV	imperfective
INF	infinitive
IRR	irrealis
lit.	literal
LOC	locative
NEG	negative
NEUT	neuter
NOM	nominaliser
OM	object marker

OPT	optative
p.c.	personal correspondence
PASS	passive
PAST1	recent past
PAST2	distant past
PERF	perfect
pl	plural
POL	polarity
PP	personal pronoun
PRES	present tense
PREP	preposition
PROG	progressive
PROX	proximal
PST	past
PVT	perfective
Q	interrogative
REC	reciprocal
REF	referential
REL	relative
REFL	reflexive
RETR	retrospective
SBJV	subjunctive
SC	subject concord
sg	singular
SM	subject marker
SEP	separative
SEQ	sequential
STAT	stative
TOP	topic
Tn	tree node
UNAC	unaccomplished

ACKNOWLEDGEMENTS

Parts of this research were supported by an Arts and Humanities Research Council Doctoral Award, a British Academy Postdoctoral Fellowship and Japan Society for the Promotion of Science short-term postdoctoral award. I gratefully acknowledge the generous support of these funders.

This work would look very different were it not for the generosity of the Rangi-speakers I worked with in Tanzania and England. Special thanks go to Mzee Leonard Mavere, Paulo Kijuu, Yovini Maingu, Amelia Issaka, Mzee Gervais Vita, Mzee Michael Andrew, Fransisca Dossa, Angela Aloisi Kitula and Mama Seba. Vanessa Nyere was my *mʊlaangi* in Preston. In Haubi, I am also indebted to Padre Sha Kijuu, Padre Sokoi and all the *masista*. Margaret Beckett and Beth Lewis also provided invaluable support and food with crunch. I cannot thank you enough for putting me up and for putting up with me.

Many others contributed to making this possible, either by helping with the work or by helping with me. Rozenn Guérois, Peter Edelesten and Andrew Harvey provided a wonderful community of support at SOAS. Ruth Kempson, Stergios Chatzikyriakidis, Tohru Seraku and Miriam Bouzouita made up my DS community, even from a distance. Lutz Marten deserves a special mention for being an integral part of both communities and for continuing to inspire.

A substantial amount of the thinking and writing that went into this took place during my time at the Graduate School of Language and Culture, Osaka University. I cannot thank my friends and colleagues in Japan enough for their support and hospitality during this time. My thanks go to Nobuko Yoneda for making Osaka feel like home. To Maya Abe, Makoto Furumoto, Junko Komori, Sayaka Kutsukake, Yuka Makino and Keiko Takemura for bringing Tanzania to Toyonaka. To Keiko Sagara for trans-continental friendship. To Keiko Ono for representing SOAS in Tokyo.

My heartfelt thanks go also to Serge for leading the way. To Sheena for planting the idea of Japan. To šdz for coffee. To Nadia who understands. To Adolphus for requesting three copies before I started writing. To Jenny for words. To Piotr for catching me when I fall. To Lucie for scrolls with ribbons. And to my mother Jill Gibson, who made my world such that anything has always seemed possible.

CONTENTS

1

INTRODUCTION

1.1. Aims and objectives

While there is a broad consensus that humans process linguistic input in real-time, the dynamics of this process are generally not captured in formal accounts of grammar. Traditional models of language often treat linguistic knowledge as static and encapsulated. Dynamic Syntax (DS; Kempson et al. 2001, 2010; Cann et al. 2005b) represents a shift in this regard and seeks to capture the dynamic nature of how meaning is established in real-time. Under the Dynamic Syntax approach to formal language modelling, linguistic knowledge is considered to be the ability to process (both parse and produce) language in context, on an incremental basis.

The DS approach reorients the set of constraints which are operative on the incremental build-up of semantic representations that result from a natural language string. Whilst linguistic knowledge is considered to be the ability to parse or produce a string of natural language in context, syntax is viewed as the step-by-step accumulation of transparent semantic representations associated with the stages of parsing and production. The representation of this process is the primary task for DS syntactic analysis.

This book develops an approach to analysing Bantu languages, drawing on the mechanisms made available in the Dynamic Syntax theoretical approach. The Bantu language family comprises some 400–500 languages spoken across much of East, Central and Southern Africa. Bantu languages often have a highly agglutinative morphology and extensive systems of agreement that can be seen across the verbal and nominal domains. This makes the Bantu languages an ideal lens through which to examine approaches to incremental parsing.

This study does not represent the first attempt at engaging with the intricacies of the Bantu clause from the perspective of the Dynamic Syntax framework. Some of the early formative DS literature considered data from Bantu languages, such as Marten (2002), which examined underspecification in the verbal domain, drawing on examples from Swahili. Similarly, Cann et al. (2005b) made recourse to Swahili data in their examination of the issues involved in agreement in their landmark publication *The dynamics of language*. A number of subsequent studies have also examined different phenomena in Bantu languages from the DS perspective. Kempson & Marten (2002) presented assumptions made for modelling Bantu subject, pronouns and agreement phenomena. Kula & Marten (2011) developed a model of restrictive and non-restrictive relative clauses in Bemba from a DS perspective. Kempson et al. (2011b) explored cleft constructions in siSwati, and Gibson (2012) developed a first account of Rangi auxiliary constructions.

The present study continues in this vein, building on previous work. However, it also highlights cases that differ from those presented in previous studies. In some instances, these deviations are motivated by language-specific facts. In other instances, differences represent developments in the DS theoretical machinery that necessitate bringing the analyses in line with the prevailing approach. In this sense, part of the motivation behind this work is to provide an up-to-date engagement with the theoretical landscape provided by Dynamic Syntax. It also aims to provide a dedicated space for the exploration of the way in which Bantu clause structure provides challenges for – but can also be modelled from – the DS perspective.

The study explores concepts which underpin the DS framework but which have not previously been shown to play such a central role in the establishment of meaning. In all of the case studies examined here, for example, the process of building and re-building structure is shown to be crucial in capturing the facts of the Bantu clause. Similarly, the analyses developed throughout this study demonstrate the context-dependent nature of the processes involved in the DS approach.

In this way, the study is driven both by empirical observations of the challenges involved in modelling the elements of the Bantu clause, and by the questions invoked by the framework itself. Whilst in many instances the analysis draws on the mechanisms and machinery that have been provided by the DS framework from the start, the analysis probes the ability of these tools to extend to new empirical domains. In some instances, this represents a relatively straightforward application of the framework, for example, with the incremental contribution made by the subject information, tense-aspect marker and verb stem as the elements of the clause are encountered. However, in instances such as the modelling of negation in Bantu, this represents a more involved exploration of the dynamics of the parsing/production process and the ability of the framework to expand to a new empirical domain.

This study is based on two central concepts – underspecification and update – that will be seen at play over and over again. Under the DS approach, underspecification is considered to be the property of natural language that allows for the introduction and subsequent manipulation of information at any stage in the parsing/production process. As information is increasingly provided, content can receive update, both in terms of the relations that hold within the tree and in terms of the content that decorates the trees.

In contrast to structuralist-based frameworks, DS does not assign grammatical significance to combinations of words or phrases, or to types of dependency – such as headedness or complementation – that may be considered to hold between these elements. Whilst these concepts may be able to be ascertained from the string of words as licensed by the grammar, they do not provide the basis of the DS analysis, nor are they captured in the formal representation employed by this approach. However, the framework must be able to capture ordering restrictions and constraints on interpretation where these exist.

The central empirical question driving this study is therefore how to account for the dynamic and incremental establishment of propositional structure associated with elements in the Bantu clause, whilst also being able to capture the ordering restrictions and the interpretations which stem from parsing strings in context.

1.2. Scope of the book

This study makes recourse primarily to data from two East African Bantu languages: Swahili and Rangi. This is motivated by two considerations. Swahili is a well-studied Bantu language and as such is ideal for discussing issues relating to Bantu clause structure. There is reasonable access to speakers and documentation, as well as to published sources. In many ways, Swahili also represents a good starting point for the exploration of Bantu languages as linguists may be familiar with the data to some extent. However, in many senses Swahili is far from a 'typical' Bantu language and does not exhibit some of the features that are found more broadly across the Bantu language family (there are, for example, no distinct degrees of past and future tense, nor does the language have tone).

In contrast, Rangi is an under-described language that has been subject to only a few recent studies. As well as exhibiting many of the features most commonly associated with the Bantu languages in terms of broad patterns relating to syntax, morphology and phonology, Rangi exhibits a highly unusual word order in which the auxiliary appears after the main verb. This sets it apart from the majority of other Bantu languages (including Swahili) and indeed from many other Subject Verb Object languages. The majority of the Rangi data considered in this study comes from two periods of research conducted by the author in the Kondoa region of central Tanzania between 2009 and 2011. Other sources, where relevant, are indicated. To this end, in addition to probing the tools of Dynamic Syntax, this study adds to the descriptive status of Rangi and to our understanding of the grammar of the language.

In many instances, the assumptions that are made for Swahili can be extended to the Rangi facts (and indeed other Bantu languages more widely), although the Rangi data often require additional refinements or adjustments to be able to accurately capture the intricacies. Data from other Bantu languages are explored where relevant. Often this is to exemplify instances in which different analyses have been forwarded – or are necessary – in order to account for variation between the languages.

The study does not set out to provide a comprehensive account of the way in which the languages of the entire Bantu family function, any more than it sets out to capture the complete grammar of a singular language. Rather, the elements that are examined can be considered as case studies through which to explore particular phenomena in the DS framework, as well as to highlight specific features of the languages in question.

This Introduction has provided a brief overview of the aims and objectives of the study. The next chapter is a concise introduction to the Dynamic Syntax framework and provides the background necessary for the discussion presented in subsequent chapters. Chapter 3 develops a step-by-step account of the issues that are central to the Dynamic Syntax modelling of Bantu clause structure and the challenges that arise. Chapter 4 examines the concepts of underspecification and update which are central to the DS approach and draws on a number of case studies from Bantu morphosyntax. Chapter 5 takes preliminary steps towards developing a DS account of some of the key strategies that are used to encode negation across the Bantu family. The discussion in Chapter 6 centres on the unusual auxiliary placement alternation found in the Tanzanian Bantu language Rangi and the development of a formal account of this patterning. Chapter 7 seeks to draw out the cross-linguistic parallels between some of the discussion presented in the study and analyses which have been formulated from the perspective of DS for non-Bantu languages. Chapter 8 constitutes a concise conclusion.

2

THE DYNAMIC SYNTAX FRAMEWORK

2.1. Basic assumptions

There is a broad consensus that humans process linguistic input in real time. However, the dynamics of this process have traditionally not been reflected in most formal accounts of linguistic knowledge. Dynamic Syntax (DS; Kempson et al. 2001, 2010; Cann et al. 2005b) is a grammar formalism that aims to capture the real-time parsing/production process. DS seeks to provide a model of the parsing/production process by showing how meaning is built incrementally from information provided by words encountered in context. One of the basic assumptions upon which DS is based is that natural language syntax is the incremental accumulation of transparent semantic representations, with the end goal being the establishment of a logical propositional formula.

Semantic trees are used to represent the establishment of the proposition and are the only level of representation adopted by the framework. The progressive accumulation of information during the parsing/production process is modelled through the growth of these semantic trees. Given the dynamic nature of the framework, a key characteristic is that it is not only the final tree which is considered important, but also the transitional steps involved as one partial tree develops into the next. The complete tree represents a propositional formula from which the utterance can be interpreted.

Another feature of the framework which will be seen at play throughout the current study is that for any natural language string, a variety of processing strategies may be available, and the specific set of steps employed makes no difference to the content associated with the distinct output structures. However, the processes chosen along the way may reflect pragmatic considerations and word order can often be reconstructed through examining the stages of accumulation and the unfolding tree. Thus, a well-formed string of words can be captured by reference to a series of trees which represent a permissible path leading from one tree relation to another.

2.2. Language of representation: the Logic of Finite Trees

The framework assumes a single level of representation which is modelled using binary semantic trees. The system of binary trees employed by DS is underpinned by a language to talk about trees called the 'Logic of Finite Trees'

(LOFT, Blackburn & Meyer-Viol 1994; Kempson et al. 2001). LOFT is an expressive modal language that allows statements to be made about any treenode from the perspective of any other treenode. LOFT uses two basic tree modalities, the up and down arrow relations $\langle\uparrow\rangle$ and $\langle\downarrow\rangle$, which correspond to the daughter and mother relations respectively. By convention, arguments are represented on the nodes on the left of the tree and are labelled with 0, whilst functor nodes are represented by the nodes on the right of the tree and are labelled with 1. The combination of the 1 and 0 and the $\downarrow$ and $\uparrow$ modalities can be used to describe precise relations that hold between nodes. Thus, $\downarrow_0$ can be used to refer to an argument daughter node, whilst $\downarrow_1$ can be used to refer to a functor daughter.

Tree nodes have addresses which enable the identification of the exact location of a tree node with respect to the root node or with respect to another node. Tree node addresses can be used to describe how to move from one tree node to another, as well as to identify particular locations within a tree. The tree node address label Tn enables the identification of the exact location of a tree node with respect to the root node. The root node is the only node which is not dominated by any other node and has the treenode address Tn(0). The addresses of its daughter nodes are Tn(00) which indicates the daughter argument node and Tn(01) which indicates a daughter functor node.[1]

(1)   Tree showing tree node addresses

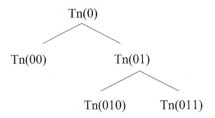

The tree modalities provide a powerful system for talking about nodes in a tree. A given tree modality might further specify the daughter node to which it refers by representing it as $\langle\downarrow_0\rangle$ or $\langle\downarrow_1\rangle$. This can be seen on examination of the tree in (2) below where all the tree nodes have a tree node address and a further statement identifying another node in the tree. For example, the statement $\langle\uparrow_0\rangle\langle\downarrow_1\rangle$Tn(011) found at the Tn(010) node reads: if you take a step across the 0 mother relation (i.e. up) followed by a step across the 1 daughter relation (i.e. down) you will find tree node 011.

---

[1] In the interest of space and clarity, the tree node addresses are only shown in subsequent trees when these provide some information vital to the discussion or which enables the differentiation of one node from other. However, all tree nodes can be considered to have tree node addresses, whether they are shown on the tree or not.

(2) Tree showing LOFT modalities and tree node addresses

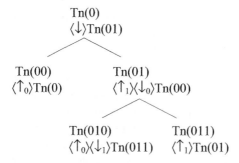

The LOFT system also allows for the expression of underspecified relations where the exact dominance relation is not yet known This underspecified relation is captured using either the Kleene star (*), which expresses the general notion of dominance plus reflexivity, or the Kleene plus (+) which does not include an empty set meaning that the node in question can be any node apart from the current node. Thus, the modality $\langle \downarrow^* \rangle$ means: 'if you go down zero or more steps across the daughter relation, there is a node'. This node can therefore be any node below the current node or the current node itself since the number of steps can also be zero. In contrast to this, the Kleene + operator does not include the zero step which means that you must progress at least one step. The modality $\langle \downarrow^+ \rangle$ therefore means: 'if you go down one or more steps across the daughter relation, there is a node'. The Kleene star (*) can be used in combination with the up and down arrows as a means for expressing that decoration X holds at some dominating node above the current node without providing the exact location of the node in question. This is represented as $\uparrow^* X$. The up $\uparrow$ and down $\downarrow$ modalities can also be used either existentially or universally. To distinguish between these two readings, angled and square brackets are used. A tree modality inside angled brackets contains an existential statement such as $\langle \downarrow \rangle$, which means 'there is a daughter node'. The down arrow modality inside square brackets $[\downarrow]$ indicates the universal statement 'for all nodes found if you go down the daughter relation'.

There is no primitive concept of grammatical function in DS. Rather these are considered to be epiphenomenal and are characterised directly through the LOFT notation. Thus, the notion of 'subject' is assigned to the content at the $\langle \uparrow_0 \rangle \langle \uparrow_1 \rangle$ t-node, whilst 'object' is applied to the content at the $\langle \uparrow_0 \rangle \langle \uparrow_1 \rangle \langle \uparrow_1 \rangle$ t-node, and 'indirect object' to the content at the $\langle \uparrow_0 \rangle \langle \uparrow_1 \rangle \langle \uparrow_1 \rangle \langle \uparrow_1 \rangle$ t-node. A final technical concept employed in the framework is the 'bottom restriction'. This is part of the lexical information of all content and some function words. Tree nodes decorated with the bottom restriction are terminal nodes in the tree and cannot have daughter nodes.

2.3. How trees grow

The overall goal of any DS derivation is the establishment of some propositional formula. The annotation that holds at this minimal tree represents this requirement and reflects the intuition that hearers expect speakers to communicate some meaningful content – a proposition. Hearers in turn use these propositions to derive pragmatic inferences in order to establish a representation of the speaker's assumed meaning. The development of information during the interpretation process is represented by the incremental growth of binary semantic trees. Tree growth involves the unfolding of one partial tree into another in which the relations holding within the trees are progressively specified. The parsing/production process takes place on a left-to-right basis and is strictly incremental. As a word or morpheme is parsed, the resulting tree state provides the context against which the next word or morpheme is parsed.

The growth of the binary semantic trees occurs through a combination of three mechanisms: lexical input, computational actions and pragmatic enrichment.

Lexical input is the result of words and morphemes and is defined in the lexicon of a given language. As such, it is considered to stem from a closed set of language-specific rules. The computational rules are available at any stage during the parsing/production process, provided that specific triggering conditions are present in the tree or at the node under development. The computational rules are universal and available cross-linguistically. Pragmatic information also contributes to the tree growth process and can provide an update for otherwise underspecified terms, both within the local context of the tree and within the broader context of discourse.

DS makes use of a set of types, primarily: t 'truth, proposition', e 'entity', and $e \rightarrow t$ 'predicate'. Two subtypes are also used: the entity type – e_s 'event term' and $e_s \rightarrow t$ 'event predicate' where the subscript s represents a situation argument which combines an event term to yield a proposition. Under the DS approach, all noun phrases are analysed as being assigned a logical form of type e, following the pattern of arbitrary names in natural logic style proofs.

The parsing/production process is goal-driven. Tree growth is achieved through the fulfilment of requirements all of which can be considered as subgoals and which culminate in the establishment of the type t proposition. Since parsing and production take place on an incremental basis, requirements can be outstanding at any of the intermediate stages in the process. However, by the end, no requirements can be left unfulfilled. It is the satisfaction of requirements that determines the well-formedness of a completed structure since a well-formed tree represents the result of successfully parsing a natural language string and must contain no outstanding requirements. Again, reflective of the tree growth dynamics, grammaticality is determined by the set of possible transitions involved in a parse, not by the final tree alone.

Requirements are represented by the query '?' and serve to drive the parse forward. As well as the overarching goal of establishing a type t proposition, requirements can be to derive some formula of a specified type from a string, to identify the function of some semantic content, or to identify the content or location of a node from information provided by context. Requirements can be seen as descriptions which do not hold at a given node but must do so at some point before the parse is complete. Thus, the requirement for the construction of a proposition is represented by ?Ty(t) where t stands for 'truth evaluable'. The annotation ?Ty(e) represents the requirement for a formula of type e (an argument) whilst ?Ty(e→t) represents a requirement for information on a predicate node. The starting point for all structure building processes is therefore the initial minimal tree which is simply a single node with the tree node address Tn(0) annotated with the requirement for propositional structure ?Ty(t), as shown in (3) below.

(3) Tn(0), ?Ty(t)

The interaction between lexical input and computational rules can be explored through an examination of the steps involved in parsing an utterance such as *Mary saw John*. A simplified account of the stages involved is presented here. Tree growth proceeds on a word-by-word basis, with the lexical entries encoded by the words responsible for the establishment of propositional structure. However, it is important to remember that the tree structure is inhabited by concepts rather than by words or morphemes.

The subject expression *Mary* for example can be projected onto an argument-requiring node – i.e. a node annotated with ?Ty(e).[2]

(4)   Parsing: *Mary*...

Tn(0), ?Ty(t)

Ty(e), Fo(mary'), ◊

As can be seen on examination of the tree above, the root node (Tn(0)) is still annotated with the requirement for a proposition (?Ty(t)). The newly introduced node is annotated with the type value Ty(e) and a formula value (mary'). This node also hosts the pointer (◊). Given the dynamic nature of the DS system, and the fact that information is established incrementally by way of multiple updates of partial trees, a device known as the pointer is used to indicate the node under construction at any given point in the parsing/production process. Pointer

---

[2] A more refined account for modelling English (potential) subject expressions, which employs an unfixed node, is also available in the DS framework. The details of such an approach are not discussed in further detail here since this example is only intended to be illustrative of the tree-building process. However, the interested reader is referred to Cann (2011) for more on this.

movement is achieved through lexical and computational actions, as will be seen in further detail below.

Verbs are defined as introducing propositional structure. This typically takes the form of introducing a predicate node and the corresponding argument node. The extent of this structure however, will be determined by the valency of the verb in question. Parsing an intransitive verb for example, will lead to the introduction of a subject argument node and a $Ty(e{\rightarrow}t)$ predicate node, whilst parsing a transitive verb will lead to the introduction of a subject argument node, a $Ty(e{\rightarrow}(e{\rightarrow}t))$ predicate node and the corresponding object argument node.

The next element to come into parse is the verb *saw*. The DS account of tense is based on the assumption that every sentence involves a higher situation argument where aspect and tense information is encoded. Here tense and aspect information are represented using a metavariable (S) on this situation argument node. A more detailed characterisation of tense-aspect information under the DS approach involves an epsilon event term in which the feature is a predicate restriction on the event variable, as is detailed in Gregoromichelaki (2006), Chatzikyriakidis (2010) and Cann (2011). Further details involved in the modelling of tense and aspect information in the framework will be presented in Chapter 3 which includes a DS characterisation of Bantu tense-aspect distinctions.

Parsing a transitive verb such as *saw* therefore results in the introduction of a transitive predicate node, the subject and object argument nodes and a type e_s situation argument node. This type e_s is a subtype of type e, assuming that the domain e contains both individual entities and situational/event entities. In this example, *saw* is responsible for the projection of this situation argument node, as well as for providing the past tense annotation for the node.

(5)   Parsing: *Mary saw…*

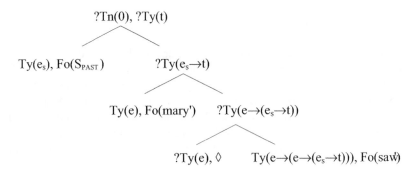

Parsing the expression *John* enables the update of the object node to a full formula value. With all the requirements satisfied (recall that requirements are represented by a query – i.e.?), the information is compiled up the tree and the tree building process is complete. As can be seen in the final tree in (6) below, all the requirements are fulfilled, and all of the nodes are annotated with type information and complete formula values.

(6) Final tree for *Mary saw John.*

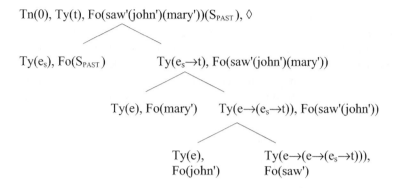

2.4. COMPUTATIONAL RULES AND TREE GROWTH

As outlined above, tree growth can take place in three ways: through lexical input, computational rules or pragmatic enrichment. Computational rules enable the development of one partial tree into another and are represented formally through an input and an output description. The input description includes information about the location of the pointer and which conditions must hold in the tree in order for the computational rule to apply. The output description shows the transformation of the input in terms of the introduction or removal of requirements, the construction of additional nodes or pointer movement. The computational rules as defined by Cann et al. (2005) are outlined in turn below.

2.4.1. INTRODUCTION

The starting point of all processes of tree growth is the requirement to derive a proposition ($?Ty(t)$). Once the initial tree with this requirement has been introduced, the rule of INTRODUCTION divides this overarching goal (and requirement) into two sub-goals. The rule of INTRODUCTION is defined as in (7).[3]

---

[3] The use of ellipsis (...) has two possible functions in the context of the computational rules. When ellipsis is found at a node carrying other kinds of information (e.g. {..., Fo(a),...}) it indicates that other information might be present before and after the information. However, if the ellipsis appears in a node containing only the ellipsis and precedes or follows another node ({... {Fo(a)}...}), it indicates that other nodes might precede or follow the node containing the Fo(a) decoration.

(7)   The rule of INTRODUCTION

$$\{\ldots\{?Tn(n),\ ?Ty(t)\ldots,\ \Diamond\}\}$$

$$\{\ldots\{?Tn(n),\ ?Ty(t),\ ?\langle\downarrow_0\rangle Ty(e),\ ?\langle\downarrow_1\rangle?Ty(e{\rightarrow}t)\ldots,\ \Diamond\}\}$$

As can be seen on examination of the rule above, INTRODUCTION has the presence of some tree node annotated with the requirement for a propositional type as its input. Provided that this input is present, INTRODUCTION introduces two new type requirements: a requirement for a type e requiring node (i.e. a node that can ultimately become an argument node) and a type e→t requiring node (i.e. a node that can ultimately become a predicate node). The effect of the rule of INTRODUCTION is the partial tree shown in (8) below.

(8)   The effect of INTRODUCTION

$$?Ty(t),\ ?\langle\downarrow_0\rangle T(e),\ ?\langle\downarrow_1\rangle Ty(e{\rightarrow}t),$$

The output of the rule of INTRODUCTION still consists of only one tree node. This means that whilst the rule of INTRODUCTION adds daughter requirements to the tree, it does not build these daughter nodes.

2.4.2. *PREDICTION*

The rule of PREDICTION constructs the two daughter nodes following the introduction of the daughter requirements to the tree by INTRODUCTION. PREDICTION decorates these nodes with the two sub-requirements and leaves the pointer at the argument daughter node. Since PREDICTION has this single tree node as its input it can occur only at the subject and predicate node.

(9)   PREDICTION – subject and predicate (as defined by Cann et al. (2005b: 44)

$$\{\ldots\{Tn(0),\ ?\langle\downarrow_0\rangle Ty(e),\ ?\langle\downarrow_1\rangle Ty(e{\rightarrow}t),\ \Diamond\}\}$$

$$\{\ldots\{Tn(0),\ ?\langle\downarrow_0\rangle Ty(e),\ ?\langle\downarrow_1\rangle Ty(e{\rightarrow}t)\},\{\langle\uparrow_0\rangle Tn(0),?Ty(e),\ \Diamond\},$$
$$\{\langle\uparrow_1\rangle Tn(0),\ ?Ty(e{\rightarrow}t)\}\}$$

The PREDICTION rule builds the subject node and the predicate node and results in a partial tree which has three nodes: the root node annotated with ?Ty (t), an argument node annotated with ?Ty(e) and a predicate node annotated with ?Ty(e→t). The effect of the application of PREDICTION can be seen in (10).

(10)   The effect of PREDICTION

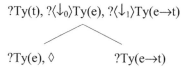

$?Ty(t), ?\langle\downarrow_0\rangle Ty(e), ?\langle\downarrow_1\rangle Ty(e{\rightarrow}t)$

$?Ty(e), \lozenge$ $?Ty(e{\rightarrow}t)$

The rules of INTRODUCTION and PREDICTION differ from the other computational rules in that these rules are concerned with the unfolding of tree structure whilst the other rules act on the values that are already present in the tree instead of expanding the tree structure.

As defined above, the rules of INTRODUCTION and PREDICTION can only apply in a situation in which no other nodes exist within the tree. However, this characterisation of the rule applies only to languages with a strict SVO word order, where parsing of the subject always occurs before the verb or the object. These rules were used extensively in earlier characterisations of the DS approach, such as in Kempson et al. (2001) and Cann et al. (2005). However, subsequent work has proposed that the rules of INTRODUCTION and PREDICTION do not apply to certain languages. In Japanese for example, it has been suggested that the full array of predicate-argument structure is provided directly by the verb (Seraku 2013a). This contrasts with the situation in English and Chinese for example, where INTRODUCTION and PREDICTION are considered to give rise to the first propositional structure and the subsequent parse of the verb may introduce additional necessary structure into the tree (Wu 2005). Bouzouita (2008b) claims that for Spanish the rules of INTRODUCTION and PREDICTION do not apply since Spanish is a subject pro-drop language, meaning that the lexical specifications of the verb alone are sufficient for the construction of the subject-predicate template.

Computational rules are assumed to be a closed set of rules and are considered to be universally and uniformly available for all languages. Following proposals such as that made by Bouzouita (2008b) that INTRODUCTION and PREDICTION do not apply, these rules were brought into question and have subsequently been abandoned. The rules of INTRODUCTION and PREDICTION are presented here in the interest of completeness.

2.4.3.   *THINNING*

All requirements must be satisfied by the time the parse is complete. Once the relevant annotation is present in the tree and a requirement is satisfied, the requirement is removed by the rule of THINNING. The input line of THINNING is therefore a node carrying both a requirement for a value and the value itself. Since THINNING eliminates the requirement, the output line reflects the removal of this satisfied requirement.

(11) The rule of THINNING

$$\frac{\{\ldots\{\ldots, X, \ldots, ?X, \ldots, \Diamond\}\ldots\}}{\{\ldots\{\ldots, X, \ldots, \Diamond\}\ldots\}}$$

The effect of the application of the rule of THINNING and the subsequent elimination of requirements that have been satisfied can be seen on comparison of the two trees shown in (12) below where both the requirement ?Ty(e) and the annotation Ty(e) are present in the first tree, enabling the requirement to be removed in the second tree.

(12)   The effect of THINNING

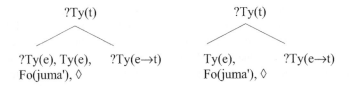

In contrast to the other transition rules which are optional, it is assumed that the rule of THINNING applies obligatorily to a requirement that has been satisfied. Although it may apply at an earlier or later stage in the derivation, it must apply before the derivation is complete since any outstanding requirements on the tree means that the parse cannot be completed successfully.

2.4.4. *COMPLETION*

The rule of COMPLETION moves the pointer from a daughter node with a satisfied type requirement to its mother node. Once this step of pointer movement has been completed, the information that a requirement has been satisfied at one of the daughter nodes is encoded on the mother node.

(13) The rule of COMPLETION (Where i $\in$ {0,1, *})

$$\frac{\{\ldots\{\ldots Tn(n),\ldots\}, \{\langle\uparrow_i\rangle Tn(n), \ldots, Ty(X) \ldots, \Diamond\}\ldots\}}{\{\ldots\{Tn(n), \ldots,\langle\downarrow_i\rangle Ty(X), \ldots, \Diamond\}, \{\langle\uparrow_i\rangle Tn(n), \ldots, Ty(X), \ldots\}\ldots\}}$$

The effect of the rule of COMPLETION can be seen on comparison of the trees in (14). Whilst the content of the two trees is identical, the rule of COMPLETION has resulted in the movement of the pointer from the Tn(00) node to the root node.[4]

(14) The effect of COMPLETION

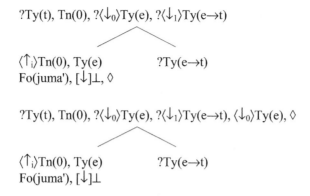

$?Ty(t), Tn(0), ?\langle\downarrow_0\rangle Ty(e), ?\langle\downarrow_1\rangle Ty(e\rightarrow t)$

$\langle\uparrow_i\rangle Tn(0), Ty(e)$ $?Ty(e\rightarrow t)$
$Fo(juma'), [\downarrow]\perp, \Diamond$

$?Ty(t), Tn(0), ?\langle\downarrow_0\rangle Ty(e), ?\langle\downarrow_1\rangle Ty(e\rightarrow t), \langle\downarrow_0\rangle Ty(e), \Diamond$

$\langle\uparrow_i\rangle Tn(0), Ty(e)$ $?Ty(e\rightarrow t)$
$Fo(juma'), [\downarrow]\perp$

The rule of COMPLETION ensures that the information from the argument daughter node is also present at the root node. Whilst the exact nature of the daughter relation is left underspecified, the rule of COMPLETION specifies that the daughter node must be of a certain type i.e. $\langle\downarrow_1\rangle Ty(X)$. In the example above, this can be seen in the annotation $\langle\downarrow_0\rangle Ty(e)$ at the root node. Since the root node is annotated with both a $?Ty(e)$ and the statement that its argument daughter is a $Ty(e)$ node, the rule of THINNING will subsequently apply. The COMPLETION rule also results in the movement of the pointer from the Tn(00) node to the Tn(0) root node.

2.4.5. ANTICIPATION

The rule of ANTICIPATION moves the pointer from a mother node to a daughter node when there is an unsatisfied requirement present on the daughter node.

(15) The rule of ANTICIPATION

$$\frac{\{...\{...Tn(n),..., \Diamond\}, \{\langle\uparrow\rangle Tn(n), ?X ...\}...\}}{\{...\{Tn(n), ...\},\{\langle\uparrow\rangle Tn(n),?X ...,\Diamond\}...\}}$$

The effect of the rule can be seen on comparison of the trees in (16) where the pointer moves from the mother node (in this case the root node) to the daughter node Tn(01) which has an outstanding requirement. The process then continues with the lexical entry annotating this functor node, followed by the application of

---

[4] The bottom restriction ($[\downarrow]\perp$) here indicates that this is a terminal node, i.e. that there is no other node further below the current node. The bottom restriction is not shown in subsequent trees unless its presence is central to the analysis under discussion, although it is assumed to be present in all terminal nodes.

the rules of THINNING and COMPLETION. Following this, no outstanding requirements remain at the terminal nodes, although there is still an unsatisfied
requirement at the topmost node of the tree (?Ty(t)).

(16) Effect of ANTICIPATION

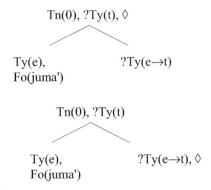

Tn(0), ?Ty(t), ◊

Ty(e),   ?Ty(e→t)
Fo(juma')

Tn(0), ?Ty(t)

Ty(e),   ?Ty(e→t), ◊
Fo(juma')

2.4.6. *ELIMINATION*

The rule of ELIMINATION applies when both daughter nodes have satisfied type and
formula values. The rule performs two functions: (i) it combines two daughters,
resulting in the annotation of the node under development, and (ii) performs
functional application over the formulae of the two daughter nodes, annotating
the node under development with the resulting formula. The rule of ELIMINATION
includes a further condition that no outstanding requirements can exist on any of
the daughter nodes. If there are outstanding requirements on any of the two
daughter nodes, the rule of ELIMINATION cannot apply.

(17) The rule of ELIMINATION

$$\{\ldots\{\langle\downarrow_0\rangle(Fo(a), Ty(X)), \langle\downarrow_1\rangle Fo(b), Ty(X{\rightarrow}Y),\ldots,\Diamond)\}\ldots\}$$

$$\{\ldots\{Fo(b(a)), Ty(Y), \langle\downarrow_0\rangle(Fo(a), Ty(X)), \langle\downarrow_1\rangle(Fo(b), Ty(X{\rightarrow}Y),\ldots,\Diamond)\}\ldots\}$$

Condition: $\langle\downarrow_i\rangle?\phi$ does not hold and $i \in \{0,1\}$

The effect of the rule of ELIMINATION can be seen on comparison of the two trees
in (18) below. In the first tree, both of the daughter nodes have satisfied type and
formula values. The rule of ELIMINATION works to deduce a new type and results
in the annotation of the root node with the information Fo(juma') and Fo(dom')
from the two daughter nodes. Following the application of ELIMINATION, the
pointer remains at the root node.

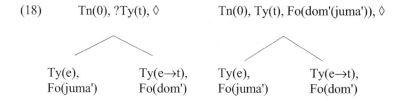

(18)   Tn(0), ?Ty(t), ◊   Tn(0), Ty(t), Fo(dom'(juma')), ◊

Ty(e),   Ty(e→t),   Ty(e),   Ty(e→t),
Fo(juma')   Fo(dom')   Fo(juma')   Fo(dom')

2.4.7. MERGE

The rule of MERGE applies when one of two nodes can update the tree node address of the other node. The notion of update in this context is defined by the tree node address entailment, meaning that if a tree node address entails another tree node address, then the former can be seen as an update of the latter. In this sense, an underspecified tree node address such as $\langle\uparrow*\rangle$Tn(n) can be updated to a more specified address such as $\langle\uparrow\rangle$Tn(a), but only when the two nodes do not bear any conflicting specifications. The rule of MERGE as defined in Cann et al. (2005b: 65) is shown in (19) below, where DU stands for Declarative Unit.

(19) The rule of MERGE

$$\frac{\{...\{..., DU, DU', \ ...\}...\}}{\{...\{..., DU \cup DU', ...\}...\}}$$

Where $◊ \in DU'$ and $DU \cup DU'$ is consistent

As can be seen on examination of the definition above, this is a very general rule. The only constraints that apply to this rule are that the pointer is one of the decorations on one of the fixed nodes (DU), and that the two DUs unify. The rule of MERGE takes place where there is an unfixed node annotation with a formula of a certain type and a fixed node requiring that type (Cann et al. 2005b: 65). The effect of the application of the rule of MERGE is the unification of information.

2.5. STRUCTURAL UNDERSPECIFICATION

As part of the tree building process, Dynamic Syntax licenses the construction of fixed nodes, unfixed nodes and LINK structures. Fixed nodes have a fully-specified tree node address. In contrast, unfixed nodes have a temporary unfixed tree node address, which must be updated to a fully specified tree node address at some stage in the parse and crucially before the parse is complete. LINK structures are used to connect two trees which are constructed in parallel.

The ADJUNCTION rules are a family of rules that are used to capture structural underspecification. They result in the introduction of unfixed nodes and LINK structures. The *ADJUNCTION rule introduces an unfixed node, LOCAL *ADJUNCTION introduces a locally unfixed node – an unfixed node which must be interpreted within a local domain. LATE *ADJUNCTION enables the introduction of an unfixed node at a later stage in the parsing/production process. LINK *ADJUNCTION introduces a LINK structure into the tree. The application of each of these rules and the structure they induce is detailed below.

2.5.1. *ADJUNCTION

The rule of *ADJUNCTION is responsible for the projection of an unfixed ?Ty(e) node from a ?Ty(t) top node. Since an unfixed node does not have a fixed tree node address when it is first introduced, it is used to represent structural underspecification. Although an unfixed node does not have a fixed tree node address it is annotated with some information about its position within the tree and includes information that somewhere in the tree a specific tree node (Tn(n)) must be found. The rule of *ADJUNCTION also imposes a requirement for the identification of a fixed tree node address on this newly constructed node (?∃x.Tn(x)). These requirements combine to ensure that the tree node will obtain a fully specified tree node address at some point in the parsing/production process and necessarily before it is complete. The rule of *ADJUNCTION, as defined in Cann et al. (2005b: 61), is provided in (20) below.

(20) The rule of *ADJUNCTION

$$\{\ldots \{\{Tn(a),\ldots, ?Ty(t), \lozenge\}\}$$

$$\{\ldots\{\{Tn(a),\ldots, ?Ty(t)\}, \{\langle\uparrow^*\rangle Tn(a), ?\exists x.Tn(x),\ldots,?Ty(e), \lozenge\}\}\ldots\}$$

The rule of *ADJUNCTION can be seen to result in the construction of an unfixed argument node from the root node (Tn(0)) which carries with it a requirement that it will ultimately have a fixed tree node address. The resulting structure is shown in the tree in (21) below.

(21) The effect of *ADJUNCTION

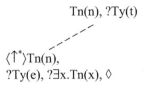

$$Tn(n), ?Ty(t)$$

$$\langle\uparrow^*\rangle Tn(n),$$
$$?Ty(e), ?\exists x.Tn(x), \lozenge$$

Given the formal definition of the rule, *ADJUNCTION can apply only when the tree is comprised of a single node with the requirement for a type *t* formula (?Ty(t)). This means that it can only occur at the very outset of the tree building process and not at a later stage in the parsing/production process when fixed structure is already present in the tree. The *ADJUNCTION rule has been used in processing fronted constituents, such as left-dislocated constituents and question words

(Kempson et al. 2001: 150–89, Cann et al. 2005b: 153–4, Bouzouita 2008b), as well as for the projection of clause-initial potential subject nouns in some Bantu languages (Kempson & Marten 2002). Once the node has been developed, the pointer returns from its tree node position which is indicated as $\langle\uparrow*\rangle$Tn(n) to the node Tn(n), and the construction can proceed in the standard way from the type t-requiring node.

2.5.2. LOCAL *ADJUNCTION

LOCAL *ADJUNCTION is a more restricted ADJUNCTION rule. This rule introduces an unfixed node which is an argument which is local to some type t tree node Tn(a).

(22) The rule of LOCAL * ADJUNCTION

$$\{\ldots\{Tn(a), ?Ty(t), \Diamond)\}\}$$

$$\{\ldots\{Tn(a), ?Ty(t)\}, \{\langle\uparrow_0\rangle\langle\uparrow_1{}^*\rangle Tn(a), ?Ty(e), ?\exists x.Tn(x), \Diamond\}\}$$

Whilst unfixed nodes have the modality $\langle\uparrow*\rangle$Tn(0) which indicates that the root node is either at or above the current node, the potential fixing site of a locally unfixed node is restricted to the local domain. This is captured in the modality $\langle\uparrow_0\rangle\langle\uparrow_1{}^*\rangle$Tn(0) which indicates that this node must ultimately be fixed as an argument node along a (possibly empty) chain of functor nodes. The result of LOCAL *ADJUNCTION is a locally unfixed node as shown in (23) (note the distinct $\langle\uparrow_0\rangle\langle\uparrow_1{}^*\rangle$ modality).

(23)   The effect of LOCAL *ADJUNCTION

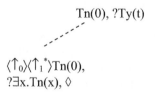

$$Tn(0), ?Ty(t)$$

$$\langle\uparrow_0\rangle\langle\uparrow_1{}^*\rangle Tn(0),$$
$$?\exists x.Tn(x), \Diamond$$

The unfixed node introduced by LOCAL *ADJUNCTION also carries with it a requirement for a fixed tree node address (?$\exists x.Tn(x)$). However, LOCAL *ADJUNCTION is not restricted to applying at the left-periphery and can be activated throughout the parsing process. Locally unfixed nodes have been used to capture a range of phenomena cross-linguistically, including local scrambling (Cann et al. 2005) and subject and object marking in Bantu languages (see Chapter 3 and Gibson & Marten 2016).

Formally, *ADJUNCTION and LOCAL *ADJUNCTION are distinguished from each other by the presence of the composite operator $\langle\uparrow_0\rangle\langle\uparrow_1{}^*\rangle$, which is used for the more restricted (locally) underspecified tree relation which is the result of LOCAL

*ADJUNCTION. Multiple applications of either the *ADJUNCTION rule or the LOCAL *ADJUNCTION rule would result in two underspecified nodes, which would collapse onto each other since they will be defined identically in terms of the same underspecified tree relation. As such, the co-existence of two unfixed nodes of the same modality is formally prohibited within DS (this is discussed in further detail in Chapter 6 and Chapter 7). The distinction introduced by the composite operator $\langle\uparrow_0\rangle\langle\uparrow_1{}^*\rangle$ however, means that an unfixed node will not collapse onto a locally unfixed node since they are defined in distinct terms – one as a (generally) unfixed node and one as a locally unfixed node.

2.5.3. LATE *ADJUNCTION

A rule is also proposed for the introduction of an unfixed node at a later stage in the parsing/production process (Cann et al. 2005a: 524; 2005b:192–221). A distinct rule is required for this since the definition of the *ADJUNCTION rule means that it can only apply at the beginning of a parse – when there is no fixed structure present in the tree. In order to enable the introduction of an unfixed node at a later stage in the derivation, the rule of LATE *ADJUNCTION is used to introduce an unfixed node after the node from which the unfixed node is being built has already been annotated with a type value. The definition of the LATE *ADJUNCTION rule is shown in (24) below.

(24) The rule of LATE *ADJUNCTION

$$\frac{\{\dots\{Tn(n),\ ?Ty(t),\ \dots,\}\ \{\uparrow^*\ Tn(n),\ Tn(a),\ \dots,\ Ty(X),\ \Diamond\},\dots\}}{\{\dots\{Tn(n),\dots,\}\ \{\uparrow^*Tn(n),\ Tn(a),\ \dots,\ Ty(X)\},\ \{\langle\uparrow^*\rangle Tn(a),\ ?Ty(X),\ ?\exists x.Tn(x),\ \Diamond\},\dots\}}$$

Unlike the rules of *ADJUNCTION and LOCAL *ADJUNCTION, LATE *ADJUNCTION introduces an unfixed node which requires an expression with the same type decoration as the node from which it is built. This can be seen on comparison of the trees in (25) below, where the second tree also projects an unfixed $?Ty(X)$ node.

(25) The effect of LATE *ADJUNCTION

The rule of LATE ADJUNCTION has been used to account for right-periphery phenomena and sentence extraposition in English (see Cann et al. 2005b: 194–8).

2.5.4. *LINK ADJUNCTION*

LINK structures are also a crucial part of the tree building process. In addition to being able to construct a single tree, it is also possible for two trees to be constructed in parallel. LINK structures constitute a formal pairing of one tree to another through a shared term which is present in both trees. LINK structures are induced by the rule of LINK ADJUNCTION which also introduces a requirement that a copy of the information encoded in the LINKed tree is present somewhere in the parallel tree before the tree update is complete. The node (and subsequent parallel tree) from which the LINK starts is taken as the context against which the LINKed tree is parsed. The rule of LINK ADJUNCTION defined by Cann et al. (2005b: 88) is shown in (26) below.

(26)   The rule of LINK ADJUNCTION

$$\{\dots\{\mathrm{Tn(a)},\ \mathrm{Fo(\alpha)},\ \mathrm{Ty(e)},\ \Diamond\},\dots\}$$

$$\{\dots\{\mathrm{Tn(a)},\ \mathrm{Fo(\alpha)},\ \mathrm{Ty(e)}\}\dots\}\ \{\langle L^{-1}\rangle \mathrm{Tn(a)},\ ?\mathrm{Ty(t)},\ ?\langle\downarrow_*\rangle\mathrm{Fo(\alpha)},\ \Diamond\}$$

The modal operator $\langle L\rangle$ and its converse operator $\langle L^{-1}\rangle$ are used to define the LINK structure. The $\langle L\rangle$ traverses the LINK relation from the LINKed node to the node where the LINK starts. The inverse $\langle L^{-1}\rangle$ traverses the LINK relation in the opposite direction. In addition to the construction of a new tree with ?Ty(t) at the top node, the rule of LINK ADJUNCTION also imposes the requirement for a copy of the head node formula ($?\langle\downarrow_*\rangle\mathrm{Fo(\alpha)}$)) somewhere within the 'new' tree. The LINK ADJUNCTION rule therefore results in the establishment of an anaphoric link between the main tree and the LINKed tree, which is forced by the requirement for a copy of the head formula to be present in both trees.

Relative clauses, hanging-topic left dislocated constructions and adverbial clauses have all been modelled through recourse to LINK structures.[5] However, different versions of the rule may apply in different contexts. For example, relative clauses are modelled using the LINK ADJUNCTION rule (for relative clauses). The LINK ADJUNCTION rule for relative clauses from Cann et al. (2005b: 88) is given in (27).

---

[5] This will also be seen to be the analysis presented for subject expressions in Bantu which in the current work are modelled as being projected onto LINK structures when they are first parsed (see section 3.1). Similarly, a LINK structure analysis is employed for relative clauses, subordinate clauses and cleft constructions in Rangi (see Chapter 6).

(27)   The rule of LINK ADJUNCTION (for relatives)

$$\{\dots\{Tn(a), Fo(\alpha), Ty(e), \Diamond\}\dots\}$$

$$\{\dots\{Tn(a), Fo(\alpha), Ty(e)\}\dots\}, \{\langle L^{-1}\rangle Tn(a), ?Ty(t), ?\langle\downarrow_*\rangle Fo(\alpha), \Diamond\}$$

In these constructions, the relative head noun is LINKed to the relative clause via a LINK relation which connects the relative head noun to the ?Ty(t) node in the tree. Whilst languages vary as to how the copy of the head formula is provided, the LINK ADJUNCTION rule establishes the LINK relation and introduces the requirement for a copy. In English relative clauses for example, the relative pronoun *who* provides the required copy of the head formula used (Kempson et al. 2001, Cann et al. 2005b).

The LINK ADJUNCTION rule which has been used for modelling Bantu subjects is the TOPIC STRUCTURE REQUIREMENT RULE, reflecting the status of potential subject nouns as topics. The formal definition of this rule is provided in (28) below.

(28) The TOPIC STRUCTURE REQUIREMENT rule (from Cann et al. 2005b:170)

$$\{\{Tn(0), ?Ty(t)\}, \{\langle L\rangle Tn(0), Fo(\alpha), Ty(e), \Diamond\}\}$$

$$\{\{Tn(0), ?Ty(t), ?\langle D\rangle Fo(\alpha), \Diamond\}\}, \{\langle L\rangle Tn(0), Fo(\alpha), Ty(e)\}$$

The use of the $\langle D\rangle$ operator encodes the weakest of all tree relations. This is a requirement that there be a copy of the term just completed on the parallel tree structure, somewhere in the development of this newly introduced root node. The application of this rule can be seen in (29) below.

(29)   The effect of the TOPIC STRUCTURE REQUIREMENT rule

$\langle L\rangle Tn(0), Ty(e), Fo(juma'), \Diamond$

$Tn(0), ?Ty(t), ?\langle D\rangle Fo(juma'),$

As can be seen on examination of the tree above, the TOPIC STRUCTURE REQUIREMENT RULE introduces a parallel tree which is connected to the main tree via a LINK structure. This rule also has the effect of introducing a requirement for a copy of the term just completed – in this case, Fo(juma') – to be present in the main tree.

2.5.5. Semantic underspecification

Metavariables are used to represent semantic underspecification. Metavariables act as content placeholders and do not represent any logical formula but rather stand as a site in to which a formula value may be substituted. They are indicated using boldface capitals, e.g. Fo(**U**) in the tree. Metavariables must be updated to a full formula value at some point during the tree building process in order for a final state tree to be type-complete. To ensure that this update happens, a requirement is introduced for a full value of the predicate to be found on the same node as the metavariable. This requirement takes the form ?∃x.Fo(x) in the case of a formula metavariable and ?∃x.Ty(x) in the case of a type metavariable. Metavariables which are not substituted as required can therefore lead to ungrammaticality. There is however a small set of specialised metavariables which do not require update to a full formula value. These include the **WH** metavariable which is introduced by a question word and the specialised metavariable **BE** which is introduced by a copula form.

2.6. SAMPLE PARSE OF A SWAHILI SENTENCE

This chapter has presented an overview of the underlying principles and assumptions which are employed in the Dynamic Syntax framework. This section exemplifies these principles at work through an examination of the application of the tools and mechanisms of the DS framework in a simple sentence from the East African Bantu language Swahili.

The basic assumption made here for parsing a Swahili string is that individual morphemes make their own lexically-specified contribution to the structure building process. As morphemes and words are encountered, the update of one partial tree to the next is made possible. The steps outlined below are those employed for parsing the Swahili utterance shown in (30).

(30) A-li-fik-a
      SM1-PAST-arrive-FV
      'S/he arrived'

The first element encountered is the subject marker *a-*, this is projected onto a locally unfixed node introduced by the rule of LOCAL *ADJUNCTION. The subject marker also projects a restricted metavariable which limits the possible substituents for the metavariable in terms of noun class – in this case class 1 (which is captured by the annotation Fo(U$_{CLASS1}$)).

(31) Parsing: *a-*

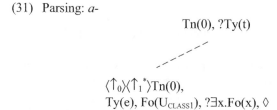

$$Tn(0), ?Ty(t)$$

$$\langle\uparrow_0\rangle\langle\uparrow_1{}^*\rangle Tn(0),$$
$$Ty(e), Fo(U_{CLASS1}), ?\exists x.Fo(x), \Diamond$$

If an overt subject NP is present, this expression can provide the background against which the metavariable can receive interpretation. However, if there is no overt subject expression, an appropriate class 1 substituent is recovered from context. In the example below, since there is no overt subject expression, the class 1 subject marker is proposed to receive interpretation from context and be updated to a real-world referent – in this case *Juma* (a person's name), as in (32) below. Note here also the presence of the pointer ( ) which is used to indicate the node under development.

(32) Parsing: *a-...*

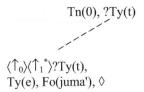

Parsing the past tense marker *-li-* introduces the past tense interpretation to the clause. In previous accounts the tense-aspect information associated with Bantu clauses was represented through the presence of the naïve annotation on the rootnode. However, the current study employs the more recent development in the DS approach in terms of capturing tense-aspect information – the situation argument. This will be discussed in further detail in Chapter 3. However, for the present discussion it is sufficient to note that the past tense interpretation associated with this clause is represented by the annotation S_{PAST} which appears on the situation argument node. The past tense marker also introduces a fixed subject node and a fixed predicate node. In the presence of a fixed subject-requiring node, the unfixed node hosting the subject information can receive a fixed tree node address and is fixed as the logical subject of the clause. The tree that results is shown in (33) below.

(33) Parsing: *a-li-...*

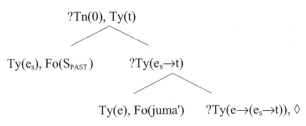

Parsing the verb stem also results in the projection of a fixed subject node and a fixed predicate node. However, this structure can collapse harmlessly with the fixed structure which has already been induced by parsing the past tense marker. Since *-fika* 'arrive' is being used intransitively, the fixed structure induced by parsing the verb stem consists only of a subject node and a predicate node. The resulting tree is shown in (34) below.

(34) Parsing: *a-li-fik-...* 'S/he arrived'

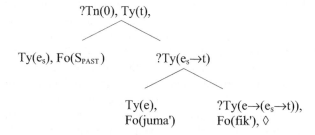

In addition to building structure, the lexical actions induced by the verb stem provide the full formula value for the predicate node (Fo(fik')). Parsing the final vowel indicates that no further predicate-argument structure can be introduced after this point. With all the requirements fulfilled, the information is compiled up the tree. The final propositional formula is a decoration on the top node, with the type *t* requirement satisfied. A snapshot of the final stage in the derivation can be seen in (35) below.

(35) Parsing: *a-li-fik-a*   'S/he arrived'
              SM1-PAST-arrive-FV

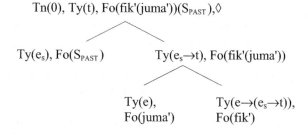

The sample derivation provided above for the Swahili phrase *alifika* 's/he arrived' follows on from previous analyses of Bantu clause structure. The basic assumptions have been that the Bantu verbal structure makes a lexically specified contribution to tree development. The subject marker projects a metavariable which can be resolved from context (whether or not there is an overt lexical subject). Tense markers project minimal predicate-argument structure and introduce temporal information. The verb provides the conceptual information about the predicate, leads to the construction of predicate-argument structure and, in the case of transitive verbs, licenses the building of an object node.

2.7. SUMMARY

This chapter has presented an introduction of the Dynamic Syntax grammar formalism. It has provided an overview of the tools and mechanisms made available by the framework, as well as the assumptions on which it is based. Under the DS approach, natural language syntax is considered to be the incremental accumulation of transparent semantic representations culminating in the establishment of a logical propositional formula. The growth of semantic information is modelled through the growth – or unfolding – of binary semantic trees. Tree growth takes place through a combination of language-specific lexical input, universally available computational rules and pragmatic enrichment. A single level of representation is assumed and all of the stages of the 'intermediate' trees are considered to be as important as the 'final' tree state.

The sequence of actions involved in parsing a basic Swahili string were presented. These can be seen to involve the establishment of local argument nodes which unify with the template provided by the tense marker and the verb. This takes place against a background of information available from context. In Swahili, the verb alone can be responsible for the establishment of a fully decorated binary-branching semantic tree representative of propositional structure. The projection of this propositional structure involves interplay between the subject marker, tense-aspect markers, the verb stem and any other elements that may be present (such as object markers or verbal derivational markers). The final default vowel -*a* is taken to indicate that the entire predicate-argument structure has been established and that no more valency-altering processes can take place.

In this way, Bantu languages provide an ideal lens through which to examine the morpheme-by-morpheme incremental parsing involved in the establishment of propositional structure from a DS perspective. Lexical content can build and annotate the tree(s), and introduce or remove requirements once they have been satisfied. Computational rules can induce nodes, affect the tree node annotations and enable the compiling of information up the tree. Similarly, pragmatic enrichment can make a vital contribution to the tree building process, with a range of information recoverable from context. The basic contribution and steps involved in the parsing process are presented here. The additional details of the contributions made by the different elements in a clause in a variety of Bantu languages are explored in further detail in Chapter 3.

3

A DYNAMIC PERSPECTIVE ON BANTU
CLAUSE STRUCTURE

Bantu languages are known for their highly agglutinative morphology, the presence of noun classes and extensive systems of agreement. Bantu languages exhibit predominantly SVO order with some flexibility of constituent ordering possible for pragmatic purposes. Subject and object pro-drop are widespread, and an inflected verb form is often sufficient for the construction of the entire propositional structure. The Bantu verbal template is structured in such a way that although not all morphemes may be present in a given verb form, the order in which they appear is tightly restricted (Meeussen 1967; Bearth 2003). Modelling the linear order of the morphemes, as well as the contribution that these elements make alongside the incremental establishment of propositional structure are some of the main challenges that Bantu languages provide for formal analyses of clause structure, including in a parsing/production-based approach such as that represented by Dynamic Syntax.

Bantu languages have a rich verbal complex. The only element which is obligatory is the verbal stem. However, subject and object arguments are commonly co-referenced on the verb through a system of agreement markers. Information pertaining to tense-aspect-mood distinctions is also often encoded within the verbal template, which may also contain elements conveying negative polarity and deixis.

As was seen in Chapter 2, tree growth under the Dynamic Syntax approach takes place through a combination of lexical input, transition rules and pragmatic enrichment. Languages vary in the balance between these types of tree building processes, as well as the ways in which these processes interact with each other. The DS approach to Bantu structure is that individual morphemes make their own, lexically-specified contribution to tree development (Cann et al. 2005b; Marten 2007; Marten et al. 2008; Kempson et al. 2011b; Marten and Kula 2011: 65). The current chapter details the specific steps that are involved in the parsing of the Bantu clause. This builds on the sample parse of a Swahili sentence presented in Chapter 2 but goes into further detail in terms of the motivation behind the analysis and the assumptions made. Examples are draw primarily from the Tanzanian Bantu language Rangi.

3.1. MODELLING BANTU SUBJECT EXPRESSIONS

Subject pro-drop is widespread across Bantu and the presence of an overt subject is generally motivated by pragmatic considerations. More specifically, the presence of an overt subject expression can often be considered to serve to introduce new information, or to background information against which the main assertion is assessed (Marten & Kula 2011: 65). Three strategies are made available in the Dynamic Syntax approach for parsing subject expressions cross-linguistically: a locally unfixed node, a LINK structure and an unfixed node (Kempson et al. 2008; Kempson & Chatzikyriakidis 2009).

The locally unfixed node strategy has been employed in DS analyses of subject expressions in Standard Modern Greek (Chatzikyriakidis 2010) and Romance languages, specifically Latin (Kempson & Chatzikyriakidis 2009). Under these analyses, case marking is used to provide the fully specified, fixed tree node address and to enable the identification of the node as that of the subject. Since Bantu languages do not have morphological case, the unfixed node plus case strategy is not available for Bantu languages and is not discussed in any further detail here. However, the notion of a locally unfixed node (without case) will be seen later on in the discussion to model subject and object clitics. Bantu subject expressions can therefore be parsed using one of two processing strategies: a LINK structure or an unfixed node.

Under the LINK structure analysis, the overt subject nominal is projected onto a tree which is constructed in parallel to the main tree. This independent tree is decorated solely with information from the potential subject expression. The rule of LINK ADJUNCTION introduces a requirement that a copy of this information is also present somewhere in the parallel tree before the parse is complete. This requirement is represented by the annotation $?\langle\downarrow_*\rangle?Fo(\alpha)$ on the root node of the main tree. This can be seen in (36) below where the potential subject expression *Mwaasʊ* (a person's name) is parsed on a LINKed tree constructed in parallel to the main tree.[6]

(36) Parsing: *Mwaasʊ...*

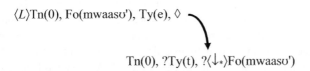

$\langle L\rangle Tn(0),\ Fo(mwaasʊ'),\ Ty(e),\ \Diamond$

$Tn(0),\ ?Ty(t),\ ?\langle\downarrow_*\rangle Fo(mwaasʊ')$

The LINK structure provides the context against which any subject information which may be encountered at a later stage in the parse can be interpreted. When the subject marker is subsequently parsed for example, the information annotating the LINKed tree enables the identification of the subject marker with this referent.

---

[6] Under the DS approach, words are not considered to address mental concepts directly, but rather to merely encode an instruction to a hearer to construct a concept which can be assumed to correspond in sufficiently close terms to the speaker's intended meaning. Such a concept may be highly context-specific so substitutions provided in sample stages of tree growth serve only as representations of possible interpretation.

Under the unfixed node analysis, the potential subject expression decorates a node which does not have a fully specific tree node address, i.e. an unfixed node (as is indicated by the annotation $(\langle\uparrow*\rangle?Ty(t))$.

(37)   Parsing: *Mwaasʊ* ...

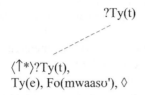

When subject expressions are analysed using LINK structures, their relationship to the verbal template and the subject marker is determined through an anaphoric relation which is represented by the LINK structure. Modelling subject expressions as annotating unfixed nodes reflects their status as potential subjects but also indicates that their precise relation to the tree under development has not been fixed and that they have not yet received a fully-specified tree node address.

Whilst both the LINK strategy and the unfixed node strategy are available for the parsing of Bantu subject expressions in general, there has been variation in the previous accounts of Bantu subjects in the framework. Work on Swahili has modelled subject expressions as annotating unfixed nodes (Marten 2011) or a LINK structure (Gibson & Marten 2016) for example, whilst the account of Rangi subject expressions is that they are projected onto LINK structures, restricting the possible occurrences of unfixed nodes to those in which the lexical actions conveyed by the lexical item encode this information (Gibson 2012). However, the different approaches that have been taken do not reflect empirical differences between the behaviour of subjects in the two languages. Whilst both an unfixed node and a LINK structure analysis are possible in terms of the architecture provided by the framework, the LINK structure account more naturally brings out the potentially problematic 'pronominal' use of Bantu subject markers (as was also argued by Gibson & Marten 2016). It also more naturally reflects the pragmatics of Bantu overt subject expressions which have been argued to be topics (see amongst others Bresnan & Mchombo 1987; Demuth & Johnson 1989) which have also been modelled in DS terms through recourse to a LINK structure. For the remainder of this study, the LINK analysis will be assumed for clause-initial NPs in the Bantu languages Swahili and Rangi.

3.2. MODELLING BANTU SUBJECT MARKERS

Whilst the presence of an overt subject expression is often optional, subject marking is typically obligatory across the languages of the Bantu family. Bantu subject markers have been analysed throughout the DS literature as annotating a locally unfixed node. This is the account that has been proposed for subject markers in Swahili (Marten 2005), Herero (Marten 2011), Bemba (Marten & Kula 2011: 65), siSwati (Kempson et al. 2011b) and Rangi (Gibson 2012; Seraku & Gibson 2016).

The analysis provided for Bantu subject markers is one under which they provide an annotation for a locally unfixed node introduced by the rule of LOCAL *ADJUNCTION. Parsing the subject marker results in the annotation of this locally unfixed node with a pronominal metavariable. The possible interpretation of the metavariable is determined by the noun class information provided by the subject marker which constrains the set of referents with which the marker can be identified. In the case of the class 1 subject marker a- for example, the metavariable can only receive update from a class 1 noun. This restriction is represented using a subscript annotation e.g. FoU_{CLASS1}.

For Rangi, the lexical actions induced by the subject marker simply provide an annotation for the locally unfixed node introduced by LOCAL *ADJUNCTION (Gibson 2012).[7] Part of the motivation behind this approach is to constrain the system of generalised rules, meaning that the step-wise unfolding of the semantic tree is the result of the parsing of lexical input (words and morphemes) and the lexical actions that are associated with this process. Under this analysis, the unfolding of the tree relies more heavily on the actions which stem from lexical input than from general transition rules. The lexical entry for the Rangi class 1 subject marker a- is provided in (38) below.[8]

(38) Lexical entry for the Rangi class 1 subject marker a-

a-   IF $?Ty(e)$, $\langle\uparrow_0\rangle\langle\uparrow_1{}^*\rangle?Ty(t)$
   THEN $put(Ty(e), Fo(U_{CLASS1}), ?\exists x.Fo(x))$
   . . .
   ELSE   abort

As can be seen in the lexical entry, the subject marker has the presence of a locally unfixed node as its lexical trigger. In the presence of this locally unfixed node, the lexical actions result in the annotation of the unfixed node with the $Ty(e)$ type value, the restricted metavariable $Fo(U_{CLASS1})$ and the requirement that this metavariable receives interpretation before the derivation is complete – represented by $?\exists x.Fo(x)$. If these conditions are not met, the parse will abort.

---

[7] This difference in analysis here is not intended to reflect a difference between the two languages in terms of the subject marking properties, since no difference seems to be motivated. However, different grammaticalisation processes have given rise to different patterns across the Bantu languages and subsequently not all subject markers are analysed in the same way. Subject markers in Swahili and Herero for example are analysed as having lost their bottom restriction, so that they can merge with complex nodes (Marten 2011).

[8] The ellipsis (. . .) in the lexical entry indicates that this is only part of the lexical entry. An addition to the lexical entry for Rangi subject marker will be proposed in Chapter 5.

If an overt subject NP expression (such as *Mwaasʋ* in the example below) comes before the subject marker, the locally unfixed node is projected in parallel to this subject expression, which is connected to the main tree via a LINK relation.

(39) Parsing: *Mwaasʋ a-*

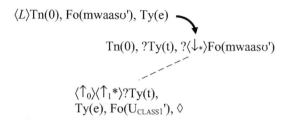

Provided that the subject marker and the subject expression agree in terms of noun class, the LINKed tree can provide the contextual background against which the subject marker can be interpreted. This allows for the identification of the LINKed NP expression as the logical subject of the clause even though its tree node address remains unfixed. The locally unfixed node is dominated by the root node but remains unfixed with respect to the rest of the tree and must receive a fully-specified tree node address before the process is complete. The metavariable is immediately substituted by information retrievable from the context, which in this case comes from the LINKed nominal expression Fo(mwaasʋ').

(40) Parsing: *Mwaasʋ a-...*

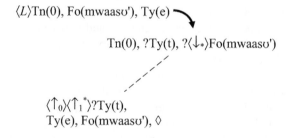

In analyses under which the NP subject expression is projected onto an unfixed node – the other option for Bantu subject expressions – the same steps occur. The locally unfixed node is projected in addition to the unfixed node. If the potential subject NP expression and the subject marker encode the same noun class, the two nodes unify. This is possible because the actions induced by the subject marker introduce the local domain within which the potential subject expression can be interpreted. The resulting unfixed node is annotated with the information provided by the subject expression Fo(mwaasʋ'), as in (41) below.

(41) Parsing: *Mwaasʊ a-...*

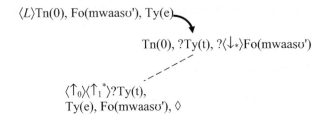

$\langle L \rangle$Tn(0), Fo(mwaasʊ'), Ty(e)

Tn(0), ?Ty(t), ?$\langle \downarrow_* \rangle$Fo(mwaasʊ')

$\langle \uparrow_0 \rangle \langle \uparrow_1^* \rangle$?Ty(t),
Ty(e), Fo(mwaasʊ'), ◊

Part of the motivation for analysing Bantu subject (and, as will be seen below, object) markers as annotating locally unfixed nodes comes from the analysis of passive constructions, where the so-called 'subject' markers decorate the object position. The locally unfixed node analysis is also in line with the account provided for object clitics in Romance, which are considered to annotate locally unfixed nodes (Cann et al. 2005b). The use of locally unfixed nodes to analyse both Bantu subject and object markers and Romance clitics reflects parallels between the two systems in terms of processing strategies – both involve the encoding of structural underspecification and the local construal of these elements in each instance (Marten et al. 2008). It also reflects other noted parallels between the referential properties exhibited by these elements in these distinct language families. However, there are differences between the analyses provided for Bantu and those provided for Romance clitics, as well as variation within the language families.

For example, whilst multiple clitics are possible in a number of contexts in Romance languages, many Bantu languages have a restriction on the number of object markers that can appear in the verbal template and it is common for a maximum of one object marker to be permitted in a verb form although there is variation in this regard (see e.g. Marlo 2015).[9]

Another difference between the analyses presented for Bantu languages and those developed for Romance languages in this regard relates to the issue of whether pronominal forms introduce a bottom restriction ([↓]⊥). Pronominal elements, in contrast to full lexical words, provide only a partial characterisation of a term that has to be further developed. A restriction on this development is introduced by the bottom restriction, which indicates that the present node is a terminal node and as such, no further development can take place. English pronouns introduce a bottom restriction since the formula value they provide is projected onto a terminal node in the tree (Kempson & Marten 2002).

---

[9] An account can also be developed for those Bantu languages which do allow more than one object marker in the verbal template. One possibility is to consider object markers in such languages as inducing a complex of nodes built from a single intermediate unfixed propositional node. This would be similar to the approach developed for languages in which scrambling is widespread (see, for example, Kiaer 2007 and Marten et al. 2008).

For Bantu languages it has been proposed either that: (i) the subject marker itself is responsible for the projection of the locally unfixed node (i.e. in Swahili, see Gibson & Marten 2016) or that (ii) the subject marker is merely responsible for the decoration of the locally unfixed node which has already been introduced by LOCAL *ADJUNCTION with the information conveyed by the subject marker (the assumption made in the current study). The first approach mirrors that taken for analyses of Romance languages and varieties of Modern Greek in which the clitics themselves are considered to be responsible for the introduction of the locally unfixed node onto which the information encoded by the clitic is projected (Cann et al. 2005).

Analysing Bantu subject and object markers as annotating locally unfixed nodes allows for freedom of construal within a tightly restricted local domain. However, the underspecification associated with unfixed nodes prohibits the occurrence of any other such underspecified tree relation before this first instantiation of underspecification is resolved. Marten et al. (2008) argue that whilst such a notion contradicts the view of the Bantu verbal structure as morphologically fixed, it has the advantage of offering a principled analysis of subject and object-marking restrictions in passive and locative inversion constructions (see Marten & Gibson 2015 and Chapter 4 of the current study).

In the analysis provided by Bresnan & Mchombo (1987), Bantu subject markers are considered to be ambiguous between anaphoric and grammatical agreement. Since Bantu subject markers are not uniformly associated with topicalised subjects, they do not have a bottom restriction. The absence of the bottom restriction for Bantu subject markers can therefore also account for the co-occurrence of clitics and co-referential NPs in many Bantu languages. This means that with one lexical characterisation of either subject or object markers, two different subject-verb relations can be modelled – with the subject NP on a LINK structure or on a locally unfixed node.

3.3. MODELLING BANTU TENSE-ASPECT INFORMATION

Bantu languages use a range of strategies to encode tense-aspect-mood distinctions. These include a combination of dedicated TAM markers, auxiliary forms and specific tone patterns (Nurse 2008). The Dynamic Syntax approach is that temporal and aspectual information is projected primarily from auxiliary and content verbs. However, other elements can also be considered to introduce such information, including tense-aspect-mood/modality markers, independent parti-cles and negation markers.[10] Indeed, this is the case in the Bantu languages

---

[10] Little has been said in the DS literature thus far on mood. Chatzikyriakidis (2010) mentions the mood diacritic *Mood(x)*. The current study does not go into significant detail in terms of representing mood information. However, for the time being it is assumed that mood can also be represented in a manner analogous to the way in which temporal and aspectual information is captured – through the use of a situation argument node. See section 5.3.2 for its application in the current work.

which employ a variety of strategies for marking tense-aspect-mood distinctions, as well as exhibiting a high level of micro-variation in terms of how such information is conveyed, where in the clause it is indicated, as well as the types of distinctions that can be encoded.

Previous analyses of tense-aspect marking in Bantu from the DS perspective have considered morphological tense-aspect markers as responsible for making a temporal and/or aspectual contribution to the clause, as well as for the introduction of fixed minimal predicate argument structure. This analysis of Bantu tense-aspect markers as introducing fixed structure reflects their common historical origin in auxiliary and main verbs (Botne 1989: 59; Nurse 2008), which are also modelled as projecting fixed predicate-argument structure (Kempson et al. 2011b; Gibson 2012; Gibson & Marten 2016). This was the account proposed for Swahili (Kempson & Marten 2002; Cann et al. 2005b; Marten 2005), Bemba (Marten & Kula 2011: 65) and for Rangi (Gibson 2012; Gibson & Marten 2016). Under these analyses however, tense and aspect information were represented by a shorthand indicative annotation at the root node such as Tns(PRESENT) for present tense or Tns(FUT) for future tense. However, an addition has been made to the DS architecture which was not captured in these accounts.

A more fine-grained approach to the representation of tense-aspect information has been developed for the Dynamic Syntax approach. Gregoromichelaki (2006) introduced a formal notion to the framework which can be used to represent temporal and aspectual information. The proposal is the addition of an argument for propositional representation that expresses the situation of evaluation – the situation argument node. Following Gregoromichelaki (2006) and Cann (2011), the situation argument node is explicitly represented as the argument daughter of a Ty(t) node on the tree and is the locus where tense and aspect properties are encoded. The functor daughter of this node is of type e but is further specified as e_s where s represents situation (this node dominates the type $(e \rightarrow (e_{sit} \rightarrow t))$ predicate node. The basic structure of the tree including the situation argument is shown in (42) below.

(42) Tree structure including situation argument

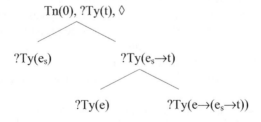

Following this approach, every formula of type *t* is said to be of the form $S_i : X$, where S_i is a term that denotes the time at which the formula X is said to hold. X is therefore the one entry in the scope statement which is assumed to be fixed independently. To reflect this starting point, $?Ty(t)$ is modified to contain one term in the attendant scope statement, namely S_i – the constructed index of evaluation. Therefore, what has in previous work been written as Tns(PAST) can be represented more accurately using indices and quantifier scope as $Tns(S_i < S_{UTT})$ (Cann et al. 2005b: 125). Under this representation, S_i denotes the time at which the formula holds, i.e. the event time (E) whilst S_{UTT} denotes the utterance time (also known as speech time or S). An expression such as $Tns(S_i < S_{UTT})$ therefore means that the reference point proceeds the utterance time and therefore refers to the past tense.

This method of representation is similar to that which has been seen more widely in the literature on tense and aspect which often makes reference to the three temporal points of speech time (S), reference time (R) and event time (E) (see, for example, Reichenbach 1947; Hornstein 1990; Klein 1994).[11] Different arrangements of these points are associated with different tense and aspect configurations. For example, tense expresses the time at which an event takes places (e.g. past, present, future) and is generally considered to be represented by the relationship between S and R. Aspect, on the other hand, describes the internal structure of an event (e.g. habitual, progressive, perfect) and can be captured by reference to the relationship between R and E.

Incorporating this development into the account of Bantu tense-aspect systems, the proposal is that a pre-stem tense-aspect marker is responsible for the introduction of basic fixed predicate-argument structures which involves a situation argument node, as well as the annotation of this argument node with the appropriate tense-aspect information. In the case of the Rangi pre-stem progressive marker $íyó$- for example, this element is responsible for the introduction of a situation argument node which hosts the progressive information, in addition to a subject node and the corresponding predicate node. The lexical entry for the Rangi progressive marker is provided in (43) below.

(43) Lexical entry for the progressive marker $-íyó-$

$-íyó-$ IF $?Ty(t), [\downarrow]\perp, \langle\downarrow_1*\rangle\langle\downarrow_0\rangle Ty(e)$
   THEN $make(\langle\downarrow_0\rangle); go(\langle\downarrow_0\rangle); put(Ty(e_s) Fo(S_{PROGRESSIVE})); go(\langle\uparrow_0\rangle);$
      $make(\langle\downarrow_1\rangle); put(?Ty(e_s\rightarrow t)); go(\langle\downarrow_1\rangle); put(?Ty(e\rightarrow(e_s\rightarrow t));$
      $go(\langle\uparrow_1\rangle); make(\langle\downarrow_0\rangle); go(\langle\downarrow_0\rangle); put(?Ty(e))$
   ELSE abort

The lexical trigger for parsing the progressive marker $-íyó-$ is a tree state in which there is no fixed structure present in the tree. This is indicated by the requirement that the $?Ty(t)$ node is the bottom most node $(?Ty(t), [\downarrow]\perp)$. However, the triggering context for the progressive marker also includes the

---

[11] The terminology used to refer to these temporal points varies in the literature, but the concepts referred to are in many instances similar.

presence of a locally unfixed node, as indicated by $\langle\downarrow_1{}^*\rangle\langle\downarrow_0\rangle$Ty(e). In Bantu languages such as Rangi (and Swahili) this constraint is satisfied even when there is a lexical subject or subject marker in the clause since neither of these elements introduces fixed structure into the tree – rather they are parsed on unfixed nodes or LINK structures (as was seen in Section 3.1 above). The restriction that there is no fixed structure present in the tree at the point at which the past tense marker is parsed ensures the appropriate linear ordering of the elements in the clause – i.e. the tense marker must appear before the verb stem.

In the presence of these triggering conditions, parsing the progressive marker *-í yó-* induces the projection of a fixed subject node and a fixed predicate node, as well as a situation argument node which is decorated with the past tense information. The resulting tree can be seen in (44) below, which shows the subject node updated to a first person singular value for the purpose of the discussion.

(44)   Parsing: *n-íyó...*

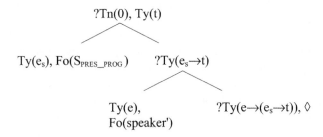

3.4. CONTRIBUTION OF THE VERB STEM: STRUCTURE BUILDING AND SEMANTICS

Verbs are a major projector of structure in the DS framework. The lexical information encoded by verbs, in conjunction with computational rules and contextual information, are responsible for inducing some or all of the propositional template they express. Verbs in the Bantu languages have been analysed as projecting fixed predicate-argument structure, as well as making a semantic contribution to the clause, providing the full formula value annotation for the predicate node (Marten 2002; Kempson et al. 2011b; Marten & Kula 2011; Gibson 2016). Analysing the verb as responsible for the introduction of fixed structure reflects the central role of verbs in the establishment of propositional structure. However, this approach also reflects structural related-ness between verbs, auxiliary forms and tense-aspect markers – all of which are modelled as projecting fixed predicate-argument structure – as well as between verb stems which carry tense-aspect markers and those which do not (for example, imperative, infinitive and subjunctive forms in Bantu languages).

An analysis under which tense-aspect markers and verbs are both taken as projecting fixed predicate-argument structure is based on a premise which is central to the Dynamic Syntax framework. Specifically, that the same parts of the tree structure can be built more than once. The building and re-building of structure already present in the tree is not only permissible in Dynamic Syntax, but in some instances is integral to the analysis and ensures appropriate construal of the utterance. Provided that the information associated with the node is consistent in each instance, the same node can be built over and over again, with the 'newly' introduced node harmlessly collapsing onto the node which is already present in the tree.

The building and re-building of structure occurs in modelling Bantu clause structure, for example, when a subject marker is parsed on both an auxiliary form and on the main verb form. In such instances, the collapse of these nodes onto each other indicates that they are identified with the same referent since the information annotates a single node. The same is true for the minimal predicate-argument structure which is introduced by a pre-stem tense-aspect marker and the verb stem. In such instances, the newly introduced structure will collapse onto the pre-existing structure. This feature follows from the standard mechanisms of tree growth and the dynamics of incremental structure building in DS.

Once the subject marker and pre-stem tense-aspect marker have been parsed, the next element encountered is the verb stem. The verb stem is responsible for the building of a fixed predicate-argument template, enabling the fixing of the unfixed logical subject within the tree. Broadly speaking, in the case of active verb forms, this will see the fixing of the subject expression whilst in the case of passive verbs it will involve the fixing of logical objects. However, the extent of the structure introduced by the verb is dependent on the valence of the verb stem and can also be added to as a result of the lexical actions encoded by verbal extensions (cf. Marten 2002). For example, an intransitive verb will build a fixed subject and a fixed predicate node. A transitive verb will build subject, predicate and object nodes. Consider the lexical entry for the Rangi verb stem *-bok* 'dig' shown in (45) below.

(45) Lexical entry for the Rangi verb stem *-bok-* 'dig'

$$
\begin{array}{ll}
\textit{-bok-} \ \text{IF} & ?Ty(e \to (e_s \to t)) \\
\text{THEN} & go(\langle\uparrow_1\rangle); \ make(\langle\downarrow_0\rangle); \ go(\langle\downarrow_0\rangle); \ put(?Ty(e))); \\
& go(\langle\uparrow_0\rangle); \ go(\langle\downarrow_1\rangle); \ make(\langle\downarrow_0\rangle); \ go(\langle\downarrow_0\rangle); \ put(?Ty(e)); \\
& go(\langle\uparrow_0\rangle); \ make(\langle\downarrow_1\rangle); \ go(\langle\downarrow_1\rangle); \ put(Ty(e \to (e \to (e_s \to)))), \\
& Fo(bok')); \\
\text{ELSE} & abort
\end{array}
$$

As can be seen on examination of the lexical entry shown above, the trigger for parsing the verb stem is a $?Ty(e \to (e_s \to t))$ node. The lexical actions induce the construction of an argument node, a predicate node and the corresponding object node. Since the verb stem in Bantu languages is often preceded by a tense-aspect marker which will typically have already introduced the fixed predicate-structure, the new structure introduced by the verb collapses with that already present in the tree. However, the verb stem will introduce the annotation – in this case Fo(bok') –

thereby enabling the update of the predicate node to a full formula value. A transitive verb will also introduce an object node. Here it is proposed that in the case of transitive predicates, the $?Ty(e{\to}(e{\to}(e_s{\to})))$ node is built immediately after the object node. This ordering ensures that the pointer is at this predicate node when the final vowel is parsed. The emergent tree structure is shown in (46) below.

(46) Parsing: *n-íyó-bók-*... 'I am digging...'

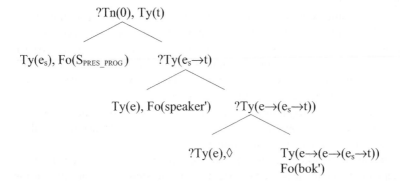

The final vowel is the last part of the verbal template to be parsed. The Dynamic Syntax analysis of TAM suffixes in head-final languages such as Japanese (Cann et al. 2005b: 240) and Korean (Kiaer 2007) assumes that the final suffix encodes some restriction on the completion of the tree. However, in head-initial Bantu languages, where the object typically follows the verb, an analysis under which the final vowel is required for the completion of the tree is not appropriate since the object is not processed until after the final vowel. Marten & Kula (2011) therefore propose that for Bantu languages, the final vowel relates to the completion of the valency-altering operations that are encoded in the derivational verbal extensions. The observation is that all argument nodes have to be built (although not all of them have to be decorated) by the time the final vowel is parsed. Since the verbal template is responsible for the construction of the predicate frame, the final vowel indicates that this process has been completed.

Following on from this approach, it is proposed here that parsing the final vowel moves the pointer from the lowest predicate node to its corresponding argument node. This has the desired effect of prohibiting the construction of any further predicate nodes after the final vowel has been parsed (which accurately captures the facts of the language) since the pointer is already at the argument node. The lexical entry for the final vowel *-a* is shown in (47) below.

(47) Lexical entry for the Rangi final vowel *-a*

　　　-a　IF　　$?Ty(e^*{\to}t)$
　　　　　THEN　$golast_{\downarrow}(e^*{\to}t)$, $go(\langle\uparrow_1\rangle)$, $go(\langle\downarrow_0\rangle)$
　　　　　ELSE　abort

As can be seen on examination of the lexical entry above, the final vowel -*a* has a ?Ty(e*→t) node as its lexical trigger. Following the approach taken by Marten (2002), the asterisk (*) indicates that the number of type *e* terms may be one or more since the final vowel -*a* can be suffixed onto verb stems of various valencies. In the presence of a predicate node, parsing the final vowel induces the movement of the pointer to the last (bottom-most) Ty(e*→t) node. This has the effect of prohibiting the construction of any further predicate-argument structure. If an object argument is present, this prior pointer movement also enables the parsing of the object expression and the annotation of the object node with the information made available by the nominal. The resulting tree can be seen in (48) below.

(48) Parsing: *n-iyó-bók-*... 'I am digging'

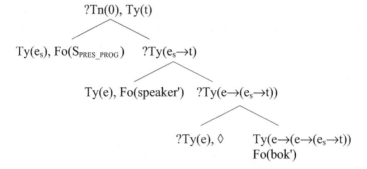

3.5. Modelling objects and object marking in Bantu languages

Many Bantu languages exhibit object agreement. There is variation between the languages in terms of the contexts in which an object marker is permissible, obligatory and prohibited, as well as restrictions in terms of the number of object markers permitted in a verb form. In Swahili, for example, an object marker is obligatory when the object argument is animate. In other contexts, the inclusion of an object marker is motivated by considerations of pragmatic and/or semantic factors such as definiteness and/or topicality. In the Tanzanian Bantu language Sambaa, object marking is generally optional, but object markers are required with personal names, some kinship terms and the question word *ndayi* 'who' (Riedel 2009). In the Kivunjo dialect of Chaga, object marking is required if the object NP is a lexical pronoun (Bresnan & Moshi 1990), whilst at the other end of the spectrum, object marking does not appear to be obligatory in Bemba (Marten et al. 2007).[12]

---

[12] For more on the precise nature of the variation in object marking across the Bantu languages, the reader is referred to Marlo (2015). Marten et al. (2007) also provides an overview of the variation in object marking in a sample of Bantu languages.

Both subject and object markers comprise a closed set of morphemes that occur in specific morphological positions, in which no other elements are found. The account developed for Bantu object markers here is based on the assumption that they function in a similar way to subject markers. Thus, they are considered to be responsible for inducing the construction of a locally unfixed node decorated with a metavariable determined by the noun class of the marker without updating the structural relations. The projection of the object marker onto a locally unfixed node means that the subject information must also necessarily have received a fixed tree node address by the time the object marker is encountered. This correctly predicts ungrammaticality in instances in which a subject marker is immediately followed by an object marker, for example without an intervening slot 3 tense-aspect marker.[13]

Here it is assumed that object markers also license the construction of the $Ty(e \rightarrow (e \rightarrow (e_s \rightarrow t)))$ node and the corresponding $?Ty(e)$ object argument node. This reflects the expectation that arises on parsing an object marker that the predicate, when it is in turn parsed, will be at least transitive and that the ultimate structure will necessarily include an object. The lexical entry proposed for the Rangi class 1 object marker $m\upsilon$- is shown in (49) below.

(49) Lexical entry for class 1 object marker $-m\upsilon$-

$-m\upsilon$- IF $?Ty(e \rightarrow (e_s \rightarrow t))$,
          THEN $go(\langle \uparrow_1 \rangle \langle \uparrow_1 \rangle)$; $make(\langle \downarrow_0 \rangle \langle \downarrow_1 * \rangle)$; $go(\langle \downarrow_0 \rangle \langle \downarrow_1 * \rangle)$;
              $put(?Ty(e), Fo(\mathbf{U}_{CLASS1}), ?\exists x.Fo(x))$; $go(\langle \uparrow_1 * \rangle \langle \uparrow_0 \rangle)$;
              $go(\langle \downarrow_1 \rangle \langle \downarrow_1 \rangle)$; $make(\langle \downarrow_1 \rangle)$; $go(\langle \downarrow_1 \rangle)$;
              $put(?Ty(e \rightarrow (e \rightarrow (e_s \rightarrow t))))$; $go(\langle \uparrow_1 \rangle)$; $make(\langle \downarrow_0 \rangle)$; $go(\langle \downarrow_0 \rangle)$;
              $put(?Ty(e))$
          ELSE   abort

The object marker has a $?Ty(e \rightarrow (e_s \rightarrow t))$ predicate node as its trigger. The lexical actions induced by the object marker subsequently result in the projection of a locally unfixed node annotated with the class information from the object marker (in the current example this is class 1) and the construction of the $?Ty(e \rightarrow (e \rightarrow (e_s \rightarrow t)))$ predicate node and its corresponding object argument node.

At this point in the parse there is a locally unfixed node annotated with the class information conveyed by the object marker $Fo(\mathbf{U}_{CLASS1})$ and an argument-requiring object node. One option for the analysis is to propose that the locally

---

[13] An exception to this generalisation is provided by infinitive and subjunctive forms, in which a subject marker may be immediately followed by an object marker.

unfixed node merges at this object node, meaning that all the tree node relations in the structure at this point would be fixed.[14] The tree showing the projection of the locally unfixed node annotated with the object information and the construction of the object node can be seen in (50) below (where the gap represented by the underscore indicates that the verb remains to be parsed).

(50) Parsing: *Mariaa-íyó-mʊ-...* 'Maria is _____ him/her...'

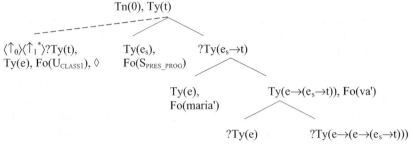

Following the parse of the verb stem, the value on the predicate node can be updated. As long as the object argument is compatible in terms of noun class, parsing the subsequent object expression can provide update to a fully specified decoration for the object node, as can be seen in the tree in (51) below.

(51) Parsing: *Maria a-íyó-mʊ-váa Mwaasʊ* 'Maria is hitting Mwaasʊ'

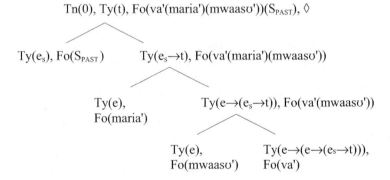

The unfixed node analysis for object markers can also be used to capture a number of the syntactic restrictions exhibited by object markers. In certain Bantu languages, object markers can only occur without the presence of a co-referring object NP in which case, from the DS perspective, the object marker encodes a

---

[14] Such an account is appropriate for languages like Swahili and Rangi in which there is maximally one object marker. However, this analysis is not able to account for languages in which multiple object markers are possible since the account developed here does not provide sufficient information in terms of how the identification of these object markers with the appropriate nodes would be restricted. This is a point which is returned to in Chapter 4.

bottom restriction. The LOCAL *ADJUNCTION analysis is able to capture this restriction, since the execution of this computational rule is not dependent on specific semantic information being present in the tree. For other languages, the locally unfixed node analysis is able to capture the prohibition on the co-occurrence of more than one object marker in a verb form since two unfixed nodes of the same modality cannot co-exist.

A final note can be made here about the role of verbal extensions in the structure building process. Many Bantu languages have verbal extensions which appear after the verb stem and often serve to alter the valency. The proposal is that the verb induces the requisite predicate-argument structure as determined by the valency of the stem in question. An intransitive verb stem will build minimal structure: a subject node and a predicate node, whilst a transitive stem will build a subject node, a $?Ty(e{\rightarrow}(e{\rightarrow}(e_s{\rightarrow}t)))$ predicate node and its corresponding (object) argument node. However, parsing a verb form which contains an extension after the verb stem can alter the valency. The addition of the applicative for example, which is commonly seen as a valency-increasing suffix which introduces an additional object argument, licenses the construction of an additional level of predicate-argument structure.[15] The same could also be proposed for the causative extension which also typically serves to increase the valency of the construction and under the DS approach, can be seen as licensing the construction of an additional predicate node and its corresponding argument node.

The role of verbal extensions is discussed here since the applicative is commonly used to introduce a benefactive object.

(52) N-íyó-mʊ́-bók-er-a   mʊ-kaaya   w-aanɪ   vi-raasi
     SM1sg-PROG-dig-APPL-FV   1-neighbour   1-my   8-potatoes
     'I am digging potatoes for my neighbour' (Rangi, Gibson 2012: 76)

Example (52) involves the addition of the applicative suffix -*er* thereby enabling the addition of an object argument – in this case the benefactive *mʊkaaya waanɪ* 'my neighbour'. The proposal is therefore that whilst parsing the stem -*bók* yields a tree reflective of a transitive predicate, following the parse of the suffix -*er* an additional $?Ty(e{\rightarrow}(e{\rightarrow}(e{\rightarrow}(e_s{\rightarrow}t))))$ predicate node and its corresponding object argument node are introduced, yielding a ditransitive construction.

The reflexive marker -*ji*- can be modelled in a similar manner as the object marker, and be considered to be projected onto a locally unfixed node. This also formally captures the preclusion of the co-occurrence of an object marker and

---

[15] The applicative suffix is traditionally described as a valency-increasing suffix which enables the introduction of an additional argument. However, see Marten & Mous (2017, forthcoming) and Jerro (2016) for an alternative account of semantics, which sees the process as more complex than simply 'valency-increasing' and Marten (2003) who proposes a DS account of non-valency altering applicative construction. This is also discussed in additional detail in Chapter 4.

the reflexive marker. Since both the object marker and the reflexive marker are projected onto a locally unfixed node, the restriction on the co-occurrence of two locally unfixed nodes also acts to prohibit the construction of both a reflexive marker and an object marker at the same time. The restriction on more than one object marker is also extended to the restriction on passive and locative inversion to which object markers are also generally precluded.[16] This approach to underspecified verbal stems and valency is discussed in further detail in Chapter 4.

3.6. Sample parse of a Rangi sentence

This chapter has outlined the assumptions made for the parsing of the basic elements of a Bantu clause. With this in mind, what follows is a step-by-step sample parse of an utterance from the Bantu language Rangi shown in (53) below.

(53) Nímɪ   n-íyó-térek-a   chá-kʊrya
     1sg.PP SM1sg-PROG-cook-FV 7-food
     'I am cooking food'

Following the application of the rule of LINK ADJUNCTION, the potential subject expression *nímɪ* 'I' can be projected onto a partial tree connected to the main tree via a LINK relation. The rule of LINK ADJUNCTION introduces a requirement that by the time the derivation is complete, a copy of the noun *nímɪ* is found in the main tree in addition to being present in the parallel LINKED tree. Since *nímɪ* is the first person singular personal pronoun, the annotation on the independent tree can be updated to a term which reflects this content. In context, this is replaced with an appropriate mental representation of the speaker, e.g. *Mwaasʊ*, as can be seen in (54) below.

(54) Parsing: *Nɪ́ɪnɪ...*

$\langle L\rangle$Tn(0), Fo(mwaasʊ'), Ty(e)   ?Ty(t), ?$\langle\downarrow_*\rangle$Fo(mwaasʊ'), Ty(e), $\Diamond$

Whilst the presence of the overt subject expression is driven by pragmatic considerations, the pre-stem subject marker on the verb is obligatory in most instances.[17] Parsing the first person singular subject marker *n-* on the verb results in the projection of a locally unfixed node annotated with a metavariable, the

---

[16] Although see also Woolford (1995, 2001) and Marten et al. (2007) for counter-examples to this generalisation.

[17] The exception to this is in imperative verb forms which are comprised solely of the verb stem without a subject marker, with the subject interpretation implied.

interpretation of which is restricted to first person singular. With the information on the parallel tree providing a context against which this metavariable can receive interpretation, the unfixed node can receive a full formula value annotation.

(55) Parsing: *Nîɪnɪ n-*

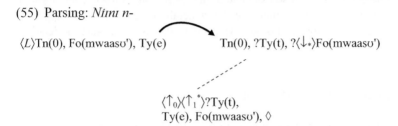

Parsing the progressive tense marker *-iyó-* results in the construction of a fixed subject node and a fixed predicate node. The presence of the fixed subject node enables the establishment of a fixed tree node address for the subject information. The progressive marker also builds the situation argument node and introduces the tense-aspect interpretation into the clause. The resulting tree structure is shown in (56) below.

(56) Parsing: *Nîɪnɪ n-iyó...*

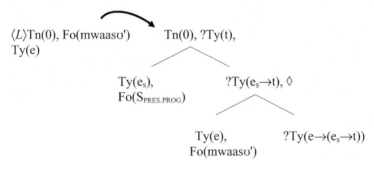

Parsing the verb stem also results in the projection of a fixed subject node and a fixed predicate node. The predicate structure introduced by the verb stem collapses with the minimal structure which has already been introduced by the progressive marker *-iyó-*. Since *-tereka* 'cook' is transitive it also licenses the construction of a $?Ty(e \rightarrow (e \rightarrow (e_s \rightarrow t)))$ node and its corresponding object node. Parsing the final vowel *-a* moves the pointer from the predicate node to the argument node, and indicates that no further addition of predicate-argument structure can be built. Parsing the expression *chákʊrya* 'food' results in the decoration of the object node. With the verb form parsed and all the requirements complete, the information is compiled up the tree. The final tree is shown in (57) below.

(57) Parsing: *Níɩnɩ n-íyó-tereka chákʊrya*

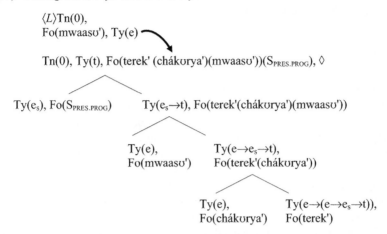

As can be seen on the basis of the steps outlined above, propositional structure in Rangi is taken to be constructed from an inflected verb form and a combination of lexical actions, computational rules and pragmatic enrichment. In instances where an overt lexical subject NP is present, this element is projected onto a LINK structure which is constructed in parallel to the main tree. However, it is common for there to be no overt subject expression in Rangi, in which case the information for the subject referent comes from a combination of the subject marker and the discourse context. Subject markers are analysed as being projected onto a locally unfixed node annotated with a restricted metavariable, the interpretation of which is limited to the specific class encoded by the subject marker. Fixed structure is assumed to be constructed by the pre-stem tense-aspect-mood marker which introduces a fixed subject node and a fixed predicate node. Pre-stem tense-aspect-mood markers also introduce a situation argument node and decorate this node with the appropriate TAM annotation.[18] The verb stem is considered to be responsible for the introduction of fixed structure to the tree. The extent of this structure depends on the valence of the word in question – an intransitive verb builds a single argument node and the associated predicate node whilst a transitive verb builds a subject node and predicate node as well as the corresponding object node. The fixed structure introduced by the verb collapses with that already introduced into the tree by parsing the tense-aspect marker. This collapse is unavoidable since the tree nodes have identical tree node addresses and can therefore not be kept distinct. This assumption will be seen to also play a crucial role in the account of auxiliary constructions in Bantu from

---

[18] The role of post-stem tense-aspect markers will be examined in Chapter 4 where it will be shown that fixed structure is licensed to be constructed, even before the tense-aspect marker has been encountered, provided that the requisite conditions hold in the tree and the subsequent restriction on interpretation is respected.

the DS perspective. Parsing the final vowel indicates that no further propositional structure can be added to the tree.

3.7. SUMMARY

This chapter has set out the assumptions made for parsing the Bantu clause from the perspective of the Dynamic Syntax framework. While some of the characterisations are appropriate for Bantu languages more broadly, the assumptions presented here are specifically those that apply to the formal account of Rangi. A crucial observation is that individual elements are considered to make their own lexically-specified contribution to the tree building process, with the tree state that results after parsing the subject marker necessary in order for the pre-stem tense-aspect marker to be parsed. Likewise, the structure present in the tree following the parse of the tense-aspect marker provides the requisite triggering conditions for parsing the verb stem, and so on. In this way, the Bantu clause can be seen to provide an ideal case study of the way in which lexical input, computational rules and pragmatic enrichment interact, giving rise to the incremental build-up of propositional structure. The tightly constrained relationships that hold between each of these processes are necessary in order to reflect the constraints on the linear order of the morphemes in the Bantu verbal template, as well as the way in which these morphemes interact with the elements in the broader clause – i.e. subject and object arguments.

The next chapter shows the application of these assumptions to the modelling of a range of issues in contemporary Bantu morphosyntax. In particular, it highlights the role of underspecification and attendant update which lies at the heart of the DS approach, in terms of capturing the properties exhibited by these constructions.

4

UNDERSPECIFICATION AND UPDATE: CASE STUDIES FROM BANTU

Underspecification is a central concept in the DS approach. It is considered to be the property of natural language which allows for the introduction and subsequent manipulation of information throughout the parsing/production process. As additional input is provided, content can be enriched in terms of both relations which hold in the tree and content which decorates tree nodes. Underspecification reflects the fact that some information which has been introduced may not be sufficient alone to determine its full semantic interpretation or final structural position. Since DS models the online processing of natural language input. Once information has been encountered it must be used and cannot be changed or cancelled at a later stage. The underspecified value carries with it a requirement for the provision of fully-specified information before the parse is complete.

Concepts of underspecification may be familiar from other frameworks and approaches. Pronouns for example, are underspecified since they provide some information about the referent, but not enough to enable their full interpretation. Rather, pronouns depend on information which can only be recovered from context for their full interpretation. In this sense, Dynamic Syntax is not dissimilar from other approaches under which pronouns and indexicals are considered to be inherently underspecified and require update. However, a key feature of DS is that this underspecification is not expressed over syntactic structure, nor is it seen as a property of the parser, rather it is considered as a core property of the grammar.

This chapter explores the concepts of underspecification and update as they apply to a number of key areas of Bantu morphosyntax. Specifically, it examines underspecification in the verbal domain by looking at the role of the underspecified verb stem and the verbal extensions, as well as inversion and passive constructions in Bantu languages. It then goes on to look at the way underspecification has been used to capture tense-aspect distinctions. The chapter will show that these constructions all centrally make recourse to the concepts of underspecification and update in the incremental build-up of structure as it is encoded through the morpheme-by-morpheme structure characteristic of the Bantu languages. It will also be shown that underspecification is tightly constrained in the DS approach, as a result of the constraints imposed by the Logic of Finite Trees (LOFT) and that restrictions that result from this can be used to account for a wide range of phenomena cross-linguistically (a point which is taken up in further detail in Chapter 7).

4.1. The mechanisms of representation

Dynamic Syntax uses binary semantic trees to represent the process of tree growth and thereby capture the online parsing/production process. The framework is based on the assumption that human beings construct semantic representations from utterances on an incremental, left-to-right basis. The DS approach is committed to the idea that underspecification and subsequent update lie at the heart of linguistic knowledge.

There are two broad types of underspecification which can be seen at play in the construction of the semantic trees and the establishment of propositional structure: structural underspecification and semantic underspecification.

4.1.1. *Structural underspecification*

The Dynamic Syntax framework licenses structure building through the use of fixed nodes, unfixed nodes and LINK structures. Fixed nodes have a fully-specified tree node address and are not used to encode structural underspecification. In contrast, unfixed nodes, have an underspecified (or unfixed) tree node address when they are first introduced into the tree structure, although their tree node address must be fully-specified before the parse is complete. The framework allows for the construction of three types of unfixed nodes through the application of three varieties of the rule of *ADJUNCTION: LOCAL *ADJUNCTION, *ADJUNCTION and GENERALISED *ADJUNCTION.

Locally unfixed nodes require update in the local domain and are represented by the modality $\langle\uparrow_0\rangle\langle\uparrow_1{}^*\rangle Tn(\alpha)$ which means that the node must ultimately be fixed as an argument node along a functor chain. The formal locality restriction on this type of unfixed node means that at some point above the present node, there is a $Tn(\alpha)$ node. This encompasses addresses such as $\langle\uparrow_0\rangle Tn(\alpha)$, $\langle\uparrow_0\rangle\langle\uparrow_1\rangle Tn(\alpha)$, $\langle\uparrow_0\rangle\langle\uparrow_1\rangle\langle\uparrow_1\rangle Tn(\alpha)$, etc. but does not allow the type-t-requiring node to be traversed, thereby forcing construal in the local domain. Such unfixed nodes can be resolved through the general action of UNIFICATION under which a type-e-requiring node is merged with the fixed type-e node, resulting in the annotation of this node with information provided by the union of these two nodes.[19] Alternatively, locally unfixed nodes can be fixed by case.

The rule of *ADJUNCTION introduces unfixed nodes which need to be resolved within a propositional domain (which may in turn possibly be an argument within another proposition). This property of these nodes is captured in their address $\langle\uparrow^*\rangle Tn(\alpha)$ which means that they are dominated by some node which may only be reached by crossing over the type-t requiring node. Kempson & Kiaer (2010) consider *ADJUNCTION to introduce a type-e-requiring node or a type e-requiring unfixed node. Seraku (2013b) assumes that *ADJUNCTION induces only

---

[19] The rule termed UNIFICATION here is called MERGE in Cann et al. (2005: 63) and Kempson et al. (2001: 86).

a type-t-requiring node in Japanese. The main idea here is that LOCAL *ADJUNCTION relates to nominal arguments whilst *ADJUNCTION pertains to embedded clauses. As was also seen with LOCAL *ADJUNCTION, such unfixed nodes can be fixed through UNIFICATION, or as Seraku (2013a) argues for Japanese, an element such as a complementiser.

The third rule, GENERALISED ADJUNCTION, builds a node that may be interpreted within any connected domain. This generalised adjunction process can introduce a node that matches in type the node from which the relation is induced and can hold across any arbitrary relation to the input node. In this way, it represents the weakest unfixed relation and is defined as $\langle U \rangle Tn(\alpha)$, $?\exists x.Fo(x)$.

The process of resolving the tree node address of unfixed nodes (i.e. the provision of a fixed address) takes place across an arbitrary sequence of daughter relations, as determined by the underspecified address. However, resolution cannot happen within structures such as relative clauses or coordination structures which are defined as projecting a pair of trees connected by a LINK relation since LINK relations relate an arbitrary node of one tree to the root node of a second tree (see Kempson et al. 2001; Kempson & Meyer-Viol 2002; Kempson et al. 2003).

Unfixed nodes have been used to model subject expressions in DS analyses of Standard Modern Greek (Chatzikyriakidis 2010) and Latin (Kempson & Chatzikyriakidis 2009). Under these analyses, constructive case is used to fix the tree address of an unfixed node resulting in it receiving a fully specified address and being identified as the logical subject. Locally unfixed nodes have previously been used in the framework to model subject and object marking in Bantu languages (see for example Marten 2011 for Herero; Marten & Kula 2011: 65 for Bemba; Kempson et al. 2011b for siSwati; Gibson 2012 and Seraku and Gibson 2016 for Rangi). Similarly, clitics in Romance languages such as Spanish have been modelled by recourse to locally unfixed nodes (Bouzouita 2008b), as have clitics in varieties of Modern Greek (Chatzikyriakidis 201) and nominals in Japanese (Kempson & Kiaer 2009). In all of these instances, locally unfixed nodes are used to capture the underspecified nature of the tree node address at the point at which a nominal element is introduced into the clause. Generally unfixed nodes have been used to model Japanese relatives (Cann et al. 2005; Kempson & Kurosawa 2009; Kempson et al. 2011). Reference has been made to generally unfixed nodes to model so-called preposed clausal adjuncts and genitive constructions in English (Kempson n.d.). Overall, various patterning restrictions and distributional properties can also be attributed to the presence of unfixed nodes as part of the processing method used (see Chapters 6 and 7).

Like all forms of underspecification, underspecified tree node addresses must be updated during the tree building process and this update must take the form of an enrichment. This means that the emergent (and final) tree node address must be annotated with a value which is more detailed than the initial, weaker specification. In order to reach this stage, the information about the unfixed node is evaluated in a downward manner through the emerging tree, in a step-by-step way until a node where an appropriate update can be achieved is reached. The fixing of the appropriate tree relation is subsequently determined by a process which unifies the fixed node with some independently introduced node, thereby updating it to a fixed position within the tree. Unfixed nodes may also have further lexically-imposed constraints in their resolution. These restrictions may be introduced by case specifications, such as a nominative case marker, which requires that the node under development is immediately dominated by a type t node (indicated by $\langle\uparrow_0\rangle Ty(t)$) or an accusative case marker which indicates a requirement that above it is a predicate node (indicated by $?\langle\uparrow_0\rangle Ty(e\rightarrow t)$). In Bantu languages, similar limits on interpretation can be seen through the introduction of restricted metavariables.

Finally, LINK structures are also available. These connect two trees which are constructed in parallel. LINK structures are introduced by the rule of LINK ADJUNCTION which introduces a requirement that a copy of the information encoded in the LINKed tree is present somewhere in the parallel tree before the final tree update is complete. Link structures are crucially involved in the unfolding of tree structure and since they see the introduction of a requirement that must be updated at a later stage before the parse is complete, can also be used in the representation of underspecification. Since LINK structures connect two trees which have been built in parallel, they have been employed to model Hanging Left Dislocated Topic Structures. Link structures have also been used to model relative clauses, where the LINK relation ensures the flow of information between the two trees and therefore, the two clauses. Accounts of Bantu languages have also used LINK structures to model overt subject arguments, where an overt subject expression typically serves to introduce new or unknown information, or to provide background information against which the following main assertion is assessed (Marten & Kula 2011: 65).[20]

4.1.2. *Semantic underspecification*

Semantic underspecification is captured through the lexical projection of metavariables. Metavariables serve as content placeholders until sufficient additional information is made available for the enrichment of the value. Metavariables do not represent any logical formula but rather stand as a site in to which a formula value may be substituted. The update of these values takes place either as the result of general pragmatic processes of substitution (i.e. from information made available in the context) or by other computational processes which may be available at this stage in the tree building process and which enable the update of these values. Metavariables are also typically accompanied by the annotation $?\exists x.Fo(x)$ which forces their update to a fully specified formal

---

[20] The LINK structure analysis also fits in with the view that overt subject nominals in Bantu languages are more broadly topical in nature (see, amongst others, Demuth & Johnson 1989; Bresnan and Mchombo 1987).

value in all well-formed strings. Metavariable formulas are represented through the use of boldface capitals such as Fo(**U**), Fo(**W**), etc.

Metavariables are commonly associated with pronominal forms such as pronouns. However, under the DS approach, metavariables are also assumed to be introduced by subject and object markers in Bantu languages where they act as placeholders, awaiting interpretation from some nominal value recoverable from context (as was seen in Chapters 2 and 3). This information is provided either by an overt argument in the clause or through substitution from the broader discourse context. The metavariables which are introduced as a result of parsing the subject and object markers carry with them restrictions which limit the possible substituents with which they can be associated, in terms of noun class or person and number distinctions. The metavariable $Fo(U_{CLASS1})$ for example can only receive update from a class 1 noun, whilst $Fo(U_{CLASS9})$ can only receive update from a class 9 noun.

The account of subject and object markers in Bantu presented in the current study assumes that these markers are pronominal clitics. In contrast to full lexical words, pronominal elements provide only a partial characterisation of a term which has to be further developed. In the DS approach this is expressed by the underspecified formula value, for example Fo(**U**) and the accompanying requirement for a full formula value $?\exists x.Fo(x)$. An additional distinction can be made as to what kind of further development this place-holding device associated with a pronoun allows, that is, whether the pronoun functions like other words in providing only a decoration on some terminal node, or whether it allows for further downward structural development. The formal reflex of providing only a decoration is the so-called 'bottom restriction' ($[\downarrow]\perp$) ('necessarily, down of me, falsum holds'), meaning that the node currently under development is a terminal node without any possibility of any further structure being built below it. Recall that the bottom restriction is part of all lexical entries of full content words, which inhabit terminal nodes, although in order to aid presentation it is only shown on the tree if its presence is distinctive.

The bottom restriction is also part of some pronominal forms. Pronouns in English for example, are considered to behave like other words in that the formula value they provide is projected onto a terminal node. This is the case despite the fact that they function as placeholders for some terms to be established from context. This means that English pronouns can be thought of as establishing anaphoric dependencies with other expressions in the tree (or those derived from context). In contrast to English however, Bantu subject markers are not necessarily associated with topicalised subjects (cf. Bresnan & Mchombo 1987) which means from the perspective of DS that they do not have a bottom restriction as was argued for Swahili and Herero (Marten 2011). The interpretation of these subject markers is therefore more loosely constrained than the interpretation of English pronouns for example, since whilst the interpretation of Bantu subject markers may be anaphoric, they can be freely updated by the two independent processes of MERGE and SUBSTITUTION. This also reflects the observation that with a single lexical characterisation of the subject marker, two different subject-verb relations can be modelled – with the subject NP as LINKed on the one hand, or as an unfixed node on the other, as per the analysis developed by Marten & Kempson (2002) and as was seen in Chapters 2 and 3.

There are also specialised metavariables which are associated with certain clausal elements, the metavariable **WH** for example is associated with interrogative elements, whilst **BE** is used in copula constructions. Since metavariables represent semantic underspecification they also typically require update before the parse is complete (indicated by $?\exists x.Fo(x)$). The exceptions to this requirement are represented by these subtype metavariables: **BE** for example does not require update since it can function as the predicative base and convey the meaning *be*, although this can be further enriched by certain elements (such as adjectives). Similarly, in Kempson et al. (2001), it was assumed that the specialised metavariable **WH** is not associated with a requirement which strictly forces update within the tree under development since it represents the question being asked and therefore represents the 'gap' being interrogated. In some Bantu languages the **WH** metavariable may be associated with an additional requirement since there are often singular and plural content question words which show agreement in terms of noun class. Thus, in Rangi, whilst *ani* 'who' is a class 1 (i.e. singular human) question word, *valaani* 'who' is the class 2 (i.e. plural human) question word. The possible substituents can be further restricted in the cases of these metavariables, at least in terms of number and noun class reference.

4.2. THE REBUILDING OF STRUCTURE

In addition to the formal mechanisms for representing underspecified relations within the tree, another key concept of the DS approach plays a central role in capturing underspecification and update. In the DS system, tree nodes are uniquely identified with respect to each other (recall the tree nodes and their associated tree node addresses shown in Chapter 2). Thus, any given node can be identified exactly in relation to other nodes. The root node (Tn(0)) is the node most commonly used to locate other nodes, but it is possible to use any node to identify the location of another node. The DS mechanism also allows for the same structure to be built twice. However, when this occurs, since the nodes will be identified in identical terms, these nodes will collapse on to each other and ultimately result in the decoration of only a single node. As long as the nodes are decorated with the same (or compatible) information, this collapse of tree nodes is harmless.

Indeed, this building and re-building of structure has already been seen to play a central role in the account developed for modelling even simple verb forms in Bantu languages where the structure introduced by the verb stem collapses onto the same structure that has previously been introduced by the pre-stem marker. This will also be seen to play a central role in the account of auxiliary constructions (see Chapter 6). In auxiliary constructions, the subject marker and the tense-aspect marker (when present) build structure in a similar way to the way in which structure is built in simple verb forms. However, in the case of the second form (typically, but not always, the main verb), fixed structure has already been introduced into the tree. In the case of a monoclausal analysis, the structure induced by the main verb will simply collapse onto the structure previously built by the auxiliary form since this will be identified in identical terms with respect to the same root node in the tree. This means that the same subject node and predicate nodes are built. Since the subject marker induces a metavariable, as long as the information provided by the two subject markers is compatible it can combine with the information that annotates the subject node that has already been fixed. The same is true of the auxiliary form which is simply analysed as introducing a metavariable and fixed predicate-argument structure. Upon parsing the main verb therefore, the structure built by the verb collapses with that introduced by the auxiliary, although the fully-specified semantic information conveyed by the verb provides update for the predicate node. Both of these therefore represent the process of underspecification and local update which are not only possible in the system, but in instances such as these, are necessary to ensure that the two elements refer to the same entities in the case of the subject markers and refer to the same event in the case of the relationship between the auxiliary and the verb. This will be seen in further detail in both Chapter 5 in the discussion of negation and in Chapter 6 in relation to auxiliary constructions.

4.3. THE UNDERSPECIFICED VERB STEM

In exploring underspecification in the verbal domain, it is also possible to consider the verb stem itself. The verb is considered to be responsible for the establishment of basic predicate-argument structure. However, the verb may be associated with different types of elements, and may introduce structure of varying degrees and subcategorise for specific types and numbers of arguments. The concept of verbal type underspecification developed in Marten (2002) provides a formal means of capturing this observation from the perspective of Dynamic Syntax. This is made possible through the use of underspecified subcategorisation information represented by the asterisk in the type value $e^* \rightarrow t$ where e^* represents the occurrence of zero or more expressions of Ty(e). This approach allows for the introduction of semantically optional expressions as part of the verb phrase. These expressions are subsequently enriched – i.e. updated – in specific occurrences of the relevant predicate. In fact, it is proposed that verbs have lexical entries which contain this underspecified content as a matter of course. Consider the lexical entry for *go* in (58) below.

(58) {Fo(go'), Ty($e^* \rightarrow (e \rightarrow t)$)}, where $e^* = 0$ or more expressions of Ty(e).

A simplified lexical entry for *go*, includes an underspecified value ($Ty(e^*)$). The type value encodes the number of arguments for which the verb subcategorises (recall that expressions of type *e* denote entities whilst expressions of type *t* denote propositions, where *t* stands for truth evaluable). The asterisk (*) is therefore used to indicate an undetermined (i.e. underspecified) number of type *e* arguments. In the example above, there is therefore minimally one argument (i.e. the subject argument) but any number of additional arguments can also be introduced into the clause. Thus, the distribution of optional arguments in the clause can be naturally captured through recourse to a single underspecified lexical entry.

This approach has also been used to model verbal extensions in Bantu which appear after the verb stem and in some instances are considered responsible for the introduction of additional predicate-argument structure (Marten 2002). Applicative verbs in Bantu are often analysed as licensing a new (benefactive) object argument, resulting in an increase in valency. However, Marten & Mous (2017) note that there are also instances in which the addition of the applicative suffix does not increase the valency of the verbal base. Whilst some of the forms represent non-productive, lexicalised verb forms, there is also a small but widely distributed class of examples which shows the productive use of an applied verb as relating to a particular pragmatic function, rather than as being related to an increase in valency. Marten (n.d.) terms this 'concept strengthening' whilst in subsequent work it has been noted that applicatives may signal that the action denoted by the base verb is being carried out in some way which is not in line with 'normal' expectations (Marten & Mous 2017; forthcoming). A similar observation has also been noted across Bantu more broadly (Jerro 2016).

The crucial element of this approach for the current discussion is that the introduction of additional elements to the verb phrase can be modelled through recourse to underspecification in the verbal domain, particularly in relation to underspecified verbal subcategorisation. It is this property which allows for a generally indeterminate number of nominal expressions to be associated with and subcategorised for by verbs. Whilst the addition of an applicative suffix to a verb form may enable the construction of additional structure, and thereby of additional predicate-argument nodes, this is not obligatory. Rather, the eventual valency of a given predicate depends not only on the structure introduced by the verb stem, but on a process of pragmatic enrichment with which it is associated (in line with concept formation, cf. Sperber & Wilson 1995; 1997; Carston 1996). This process of pragmatic enrichment establishes the occasion-specific meaning of an expression with recourse to information that is provided by the lexicon-specific information, as well as broader world/contextual information.

This approach has been seen in the current study in relation to the account of applicative constructions in Rangi, particularly those associated with an object marker (see Chapter 3). For Rangi, it was proposed that parsing the default final vowel in the verb stems results in movement of the pointer from the lowest predicate node to its corresponding argument node. This has the effect of prohibiting the construction of any further predicate nodes after the construction of the bottom-most node, since the pointer is already at the argument node. As can be seen in (59) below, the lexical entry for the final vowel hinges on the underspecified nature of the verb stem which is captured by recourse to $Ty(e^* \to t)$.

(59) Lexical entry for the Rangi final vowel *-a* (repeated from (47) above)

$$-a \quad \text{IF} \quad ?Ty(e^* \to t)$$
$$\qquad \text{THEN} \qquad golast(e^* \to t), \, go(\langle \uparrow_1 \rangle); \, go(\langle \downarrow_0 \rangle);$$
$$\qquad \text{ELSE} \qquad \text{abort}$$

The use of the underspecified verb stem is crucial to the parsing of the final vowel, since the verb form parsed before the final vowel is encountered could be of any valency and the lexical actions triggered by parsing the final vowel have to occur regardless of the transitivity of the verb. Verb stems are therefore considered to introduce $Ty(e^* \to t)$ nodes. The extent of structure is determined through context and in conjunction with the valency-alternating verbal extensions that may be present. In the case of verbs with explicit valency-altering extensions, these extensions are considered responsible for the construction of additional predicate-argument structure. However, in the case of verb stems which could function intransitively or transitively (*-doma* 'go' for example) the extent of structure is established through pragmatic enrichment. Recall that in the DS approach, information once introduced cannot be undone and the parse must progress monotonically. However, for any given string there may be multiple parsing strategies available. Therefore, a predicate such as *-doma* 'go' can be parsed both in a way that allows the subsequent construction of further structure (if it is followed by an object argument) or allows for the one-place predicate to be the point at which the parse ends. In this way, underspecification, right down to the extent of structure built by the verb, is central to the DS approach.

4.4. UNDERSPECIFIED TEMPORAL DISTINCTIONS

Chapter 3 presented an account of pre-stem tense-aspect markers in Bantu and the way in which these contribute to the structure building process. Markers which appear before the verb stem are considered to induce the construction of fixed predicate-argument structure, reflecting their common historical origin in auxiliary and main verbs (Botne 1989: 59; Nurse 2008), which are also modelled as introducing fixed structure (Kempson et al. 2011b; Gibson 2012; Gibson & Marten 2016). The Bantu pre-stem tense-aspect markers also introduce a situation argument node, on to which the tense-aspect information with which they are associated is projected.

In addition to the tense-aspect markers which appear before the verb stem, a number of Bantu languages use tense-aspect markers after the verb stem to encode temporal, aspectual and mood distinctions (Nurse & Philippson 2006; Nurse 2008). Such markers pose a challenge for the account of Bantu clause structure which has been developed so far (over the course of Chapters 2 and 3). This is, in part, due to the 'delay' in the introduction of the semantic contribution made by these markers (i.e. the tense-aspect information with which they are associated). But also, because, under the approach developed so far, it is the tense-aspect markers which introduce the first fixed structure into the tree building process. It is the presence of this fixed structure which enables the subsequent parse of the verb stem which was modelled as having a $?Ty(e \rightarrow (e_s \rightarrow t))$ node as its lexical trigger. Remember that the DS approach is strictly linear and must proceed on a left-to-right basis as choices are made in an online manner. The question is therefore how best to account for the unfolding of the structure associated with verbs in Bantu languages which have post-stem tense-aspect markers.

Whilst Standard Swahili does not have post-stem tense-aspect markers, this is not the case for a wide range of other Bantu languages which employ these forms throughout their tense-aspect systems, either in addition to pre-stem markers or instead of prefixes. This can be seen on examination of the example from Bemba in (60) below.

(60) bá-fîk-île   maílo
     SM2-arrive-PERF   yesterday
     'they arrived yesterday' (Bemba, Kula & Marten 2011: 65)

In order to tackle the challenge posed by such TAM suffixes, Marten and Kula (2011) propose an approach in which pre-stem tense-aspect markers license the establishment of structure which anticipates a specific tense-aspect interpretation before this information is actually induced. For the perfective suffix *-ile* in Bemba for example, they propose that the construction of a fixed subject node and a fixed predicate node is licensed after the subject marker has been parsed, even in the absence of a pre-stem marker. However, this option is dependent on the requirement that the eventual interpretation of the clause will be perfective. This is captured by the introduction of the requirement for the perfective reading ($?Tns(PERF)$) into the tree at the point where this structure is built. For Bemba, this requirement for the perfective interpretation is fulfilled when the suffix is parsed and the Tns(PERF) annotation is introduced. Following the parse of the suffix *-ile*, the partial tree can either be further developed or completed since the tense requirement has been satisfied. As with all other requirements, if the tense requirement is not satisfied, the tree growth cannot proceed.

In Bemba, the anticipatory building of structure is therefore restricted to the perfective verb forms in which tense marking appears after the verb root. In order for this analysis to be possible however, the contexts in which this can occur must also be highly constrained. The account developed for Bemba therefore relies on the fact that the language has only one form which appears without a pre-stem tense-aspect marker – the perfective – in order for the appropriate building of tree structure and the subsequent interpretation to be permissible. This therefore represents underspecification in the temporal domain, but is reflected through possible transitions in the tree building process which rely on the highly restricted eventual interpretation of this underspecification. Thus, whilst pre-stem tense-aspect markers induce fixed predicate argument structure and their associated tense-aspect interpretation, tense-aspect suffixes do not introduce fixed predicate-argument structure into the tree, they are responsible only for the induction of the relevant tense-aspect information, the requirement for which has already been introduced into the tree.

The approach adopted by Marten & Kula (2011) was also employed by Gibson (2012) to account for tense-aspect suffixes in Rangi. The facts of the Rangi tense-aspect system are slightly different from those of the Bemba system. In Rangi the contexts in which a tense-aspect suffix is found are not restricted to just one context and are also associated with the presence of a pre-stem marker which appears either with a low tone or a high tone: *a-* or *á-*. As can be seen on examination of the Table 1, the prefix *a-* is not associated with a single specific tense-aspect distinction.

As can be seen on examination of Table 1, the general present, habitual and distant past forms are all associated with the pre-stem marker *a-* whilst the recent past, perfective and recent past habitual are associated with the pre-stem marker *á-*.[21]

The proposal is that the pre-stem marker *a-* results in the projection of fixed minimal predicate argument structure in Rangi (Gibson 2012). The pre-stem marker can therefore be considered responsible for introducing the $?Ty(e{\rightarrow}t)$ node. This has the desired effect of ensuring that fixed structure is present in the tree at the point at which the verb stem is parsed. In terms of the temporal and/or aspectual interpretation of the clause, *a-* and *á-* are analysed as introducing a

Table 1. Rangi simple verb forms employing pre- and post-stem marking

Tense-aspect	Form
General present	SM-a-STEM-a
Habitual	SM-a-STEM-aa
Distant past	SM-a-STEM-á
Recent past	SM-á-STEM-iré
Perfective	SM-a-STEM-ire
Recent past habitual	SM-á-STEM-áá

[21] Little has been said about tone up to this point, although it plays a role in the formation of these specific tense-aspect combinations. Grammatical tone in Rangi is assumed to function in the same way as any segmental morphology and make a contribution to the tree under development. In the context in which a tone pattern is associated with a specific tense-aspect contribution, this will simply lead to the introduction of this information into the situation argument node. Lexical tone simply determines the lexical contribution of the element to the parse.

restriction that the temporal interpretation is simply non-future. This reflects the observation that although the pre-stem markers *a-* and *á-* are used in a range of tense-aspect combinations, none of these are associated with a future tense interpretation. Although this pre-stem marker *a-* is therefore not responsible for the introduction of a specific tense or aspect interpretation, it reduces the possible interpretations with which the eventual clause can be associated. When the tense-aspect suffix is subsequently parsed, this narrows down the possible interpretations and enables the update of the situation argument node annotation to a full value. In the case of the suffix *-ire* for example, the perfective information is introduced to the tree, whilst in the case of the suffix *-áa* the ultimate interpretation is recent past habitual.

However, this approach does not make reference to the situation argument node in the process of representing tense-aspect information. Under the account in which the situation argument node is used as the locus for tense-aspect information, this pre-stem marker in Rangi can be considered to also be responsible for the introduction of the situation argument node into the tree, as well as for the building of the basic predicate-argument skeletal structure. It is therefore not necessary to propose that the pre-stem marker introduces a particular restriction in terms of interpretation into the tree (as was proposed for ? Tns(PERF) for example). Rather, since the pre-stem marker can be considered to induce the requisite structure to enable the parsing of the verb stem, the parse can continue in the standard way, with the pre-stem marker inducing fixed structure and the verb stem subsequently being parsed. The specific tense-aspect interpretation that obtains in these constructions can therefore be seen to be encoded in the lexical entry of the tense-aspect suffixes, with this representing semantic (rather than structural) underspecification.

Consider the recent past habitual form shown in (61) below.

(61) ha-ra   ha-antʊ   h-á-vir-w-áa   vi-ryo
     16-DEM   16-place   SM16-PAST1-hit-PASS-HAB   8-millet
     'The place where millet was beaten' (Gibson 2012: 67)

This form is constructed through the combination of the recent past prefix *á-* and the habitual suffix *-áa*, and can therefore be proposed to induce the construction of the situation argument node and to provide the recent past tense annotation for this node. Parsing the suffix provides the aspectual information which annotates the situation argument node, but makes no other structural contribution to the tree.

However, not all forms in the Bantu tense-aspect systems are as fully compositional as that shown in (61) above. The pre-stem marker *a-* for example, is used in the formation of past tense constructions, but also appears as part of the verb form in the general present tense and the present tense habitual. The different interpretations that are found with these three forms are the result of the combination of the prefix and the suffix. Thus, whilst they all employ the prefix *a-*, the distant past employs the suffix *á-*, the general present involves the suffix

-*a* and the habitual form hosts the suffix -*aa*. It is therefore not only the lexical entry of the prefix *a*- which determines the resulting tense-aspect information, but rather the lexical actions induced as a result of parsing these suffixes in the specific parsing context – in this case, in the presence of the prefix *a*-. In this sense, the tense-aspect suffixes are also highly context-dependent and rely on the introduction of an underspecified value by the prefix *a*- before they can provide a more enriched value for the situation argument node. The prefix *a*- could therefore be modelled as encoding simply a requirement for any kind of tense-aspect information to be introduced (i.e. a general requirement ?Tns(x), ?Asp(x)). However, such a restriction is not necessary, and the lexical actions triggered by parsing the suffixes can be considered alone sufficient for capturing the specific tense-aspect interpretations that obtain.

Finally, in addition to introducing specific temporal and aspectual information into the parse, these suffixes also serve an additional procedural function, which is to indicate that the end of the verbal template has been reached and that no further predicate structure can be introduced. These post-stem tense-aspect suffixes can therefore be analysed as moving the pointer from the lowest predicate node to its associated argument node, in the same way that the 'final vowel' -*a* is analysed (see Section 3.4). In doing so, it indicates that no additional predicate or argument nodes can be constructed.

This account is also in line with the observations made in relation to parsing incrementality in Korean which Kiaer (2005) describes as 'pro-active'. Under this approach, the parsing is considered to update the emergent structure by anticipating future structure. This structure building can take place far in advance of the actual morphological material being encountered or at the point where the structure could be determined solely on a lexical basis.

The DS approach to underspecification in the temporal domain has parallels to proposals made by, amongst others Partee (1973), Kamp & Reyle (1993) and Perrett (1996, 2000) who consider all temporal expressions to be to some extent underspecified and to depend on contextual enrichment for their interpretation. Indeed, the reference to underspecification in the temporal domain in the DS approach is not intended to conflict with this approach or to suggest that this is the first or only such occasion that such a proposal has been made. However, what is important here is the use of standard DS devices for representing underspecification – the introduction of a restriction (or a requirement) on some otherwise highly underspecified element of the clause, in order to represent the incremental establishment of structure. Under the DS approach, as more and more morphemes or words are parsed, less and less future options are available for the unfolding pathway of the parse. To put it in other words, at the outset, when the tree consists of only ?Ty(t) everything is possible. However, as the morphemes are parsed on a strictly left-to-right basis, their contribution enables the information to be manipulated and increasingly enriched tree relations emerge. However, this goes hand in hand with the narrowing down of options and the possible manipulation of content, the very definition of underspecification.

4.5. Underspecification and variant constituent order

4.5.1. *Bantu inversion constructions*

A relatively widespread phenomenon across the Bantu language family is the presence of inversion constructions. These constructions all involve deviation from a more typical word order to some extent. Common types of inversion constructions involve locative inversion, patient inversion (also known as subject-object reversal), semantic locative inversion and instrument inversion. These constructions differ in terms of the thematic properties of the nouns involved, as well as the agreement triggered. However, they are united by the following four characteristics: (i) the logical subject follows the verb and is obligatorily present; (ii) the post-verbal subject is non-topical; (iii) object marking is prohibited; and (iv) there is a close relationship between the verb and the post-verbal nominal (with no intonation breaks etc. between the two elements) (Marten & van der Wal 2015).

Building on from the analysis of the more typical Bantu clause structure presented in Chapter 3, these construction types provide a number of interesting challenges for the DS approach. The first issue relates to accurately capturing the order of the elements in the clause. Whilst in a non-inverted simple clause, the first nominal phrase (when present) is both the logical and syntactic object, this is not always the case in inversion constructions, particularly in subject-object reversal for example, where the pre-verbal nominal is not construed as the subject. Similarly, in some inversion constructions, the order in which the associated structure is built deviates from that seen in the more typical Bantu clauses (as will be shown below). The issue of how to ensure the requisite structure is in place to provide the necessary triggering conditions for the following element therefore arises. A similar challenge relates to how to ensure the correct interpretation with inversion constructions. This is due to the fact that with different agreement patterns and nominal placement, certain readings, whilst being possible in structural terms, are not possible interpretations in real-world terms. Finally, there is the challenge of capturing the semantic-pragmatic interpretational properties with which the inversion constructions are associated. As their name suggests, these constructions all involve an inverted constituent order. However, this deviation from the canonical ordering carries with it specific information structural properties. Therefore, any comprehensive account of these structures would need to be able to also account for the pragmatic effects of their use.

Marten & Gibson (2016) propose that a unified account of Bantu inversion constructions can be developed. They examine locative inversion, subject-object reversal, semantic locative inversion and instrument inversion across a number of Bantu languages. The details of the distributional properties and the interpretations with which all of these constructions are associated are beyond the scope of the current study. However, the interested reader is referred to Marten & Gibson (2016) for the details of the formal account and Marten & van der Wal (2015) for a typology of inversion constructions across the Bantu language family. The key elements for the current discussion involve the formal means employed to represent these constructions, which draw heavily on the concepts of underspecification and update.

In structural terms, all of the types of inversion construction are proposed to involve: (i) the projection of the pre-verbal NP onto a LINK structure at the outset of the parse – providing the context against which the rest of the clause can be parsed; (ii) the construction of a locally unfixed node onto which the information from the potential/putative 'subject marker' is projected; and (iii) the pragmatic effects associated with the post-verbal noun phrase being attributed to the 'late' merge of this nominal. Whilst the accounts of all types of Bantu clause structure involve at least some reference to the notions of underspecification and update, the projection of the locally unfixed node will be seen to be particularly relevant for the current discussion. This will be explored here with a view to further understanding the broad nature of underspecification and update. However, in these constructions a key notion will be the observation that although update may be available at some given point in the parse, this update does not have to occur as soon as the necessary information is present in the tree.

The first type of inversion construction examined here is patient inversion. Patient inversion (also known as subject-object reversal) involves the patient appearing before the verb, thereby triggering agreement with the patient, whilst the logical subject appears immediately post-verbally. This can be seen on examination of the examples below from Swahili.

(62) M-lima u-me-pand-a   wa-tu
      3-hill SM3-PRF-climb-FV 2-person
      'People have climbed the hill.'
      lit.: 'The hill has climbed the people.'
                              (Swahili, Whiteley & Mganga 1969: 115)

(63) Wimbo   u-ta-imb-a   wa-tu   mia.
      11.song SM11-FUT-sing-FV 2-person hundred
      'A hundred people will sing the song.'
      (lit.: The song will sing a hundred people)
                              (Swahili, Whiteley & Mganga 1969: 113)

In examples (62) and (63) above, the crucial information to consider is the subject marking properties. Whilst Bantu languages exhibit a relatively free word order (particularly in instances in which there is an object marker on the verb), the examples above do not show dislocated nominal phrases but rather an 'inversion' in the order of arguments. Crucially, this is indicated through the agreement which is triggered, with the verb agreeing with the pre-verbal noun phrase. Thus, example (62) can be translated literally as 'the hill has climbed the people' although the interpretation is 'the people climbed the hill'.

The proposal developed in Marten & Gibson (2016) is that the pre-verbal nominal expression is projected onto a LINK structure or an unfixed node. In line with the approach that has been seen throughout the current study, the pre-verbal expression is considered to be projected onto a LINK structure and the subject marker is projected onto a locally unfixed node. The subject marker can be interpreted against the backdrop of the value on the LINK structure and subsequently the locally unfixed node is annotated with this value Fo(mlima'). The pre-stem tense marker is the next element to be parsed. It introduces a situation argument node annotated with the perfective information and a fixed skeletal predicate-argument structure. This is the point at which the crucial difference between 'standard' sentences and inversion constructions emerges. Whilst the locally unfixed node annotated with *mlima* 'mountain' can merge with the fixed subject node, it does not have to. Recall that multiple strategies may be available for the parsing of a single natural language string. Thus, whilst this locally unfixed node can merge at this point, there is nothing that forces this merge to happen. The analysis developed for patient inversion in Swahili therefore crucially hinges on the fact that the locally unfixed node does not merge at this point (in order to capture the interpretation with which this construction is associated) and that this underspecified tree relation persists until a later point in the tree building process.

The verb stem is subsequently parsed, resulting in the introduction of more fixed predicate-argument structure and the lexico-semantic information to annotate the predicate node. However, the node annotated with the information from the pre-verbal nominal phrase is still unfixed. The account developed by Marten & Gibson (2016) is that although in structural terms the locally unfixed node could merge at the subject node, this would result in a semantically implausible 'fairy tale' reading, i.e. that the hill climbed the people. Since the reading that hills are agents is an unlikely interpretation, it is proposed that the locally unfixed node merges instead at the 'object' position, as can be seen in the tree below.

(64)   Parsing: *Mlima u-me-panda...*

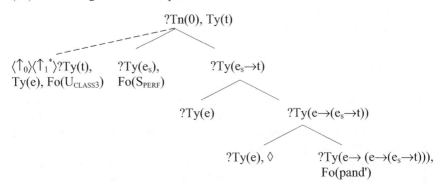

Since the locally unfixed node merges at the object position, this means that the requirement on the Ty(e) subject node is still present at this point. Semantic information is compiled up the tree and through the application of the rule of ANTICIPATION (since the subject node needs to receive an annotation), the pointer returns to the type-e-requiring subject node. The only possible way for this outstanding requirement to be satisfied is with the information from the post-verbal nominal phrase which is the next element to be parsed and which provides the annotation for this node.

(65) Parsing: *Mlima u-me-panda watu* 'People climbed the mountain'

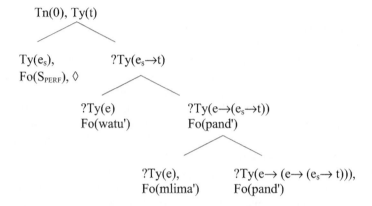

This analysis also reflects a distributional feature of inversion constructions in many Bantu languages. Whilst the omission of subject and object arguments is widespread across Bantu, in inversion constructions, the post-verbal nominal phrase cannot be omitted. Under this analysis, the obligatory presence of the logical subject can be accounted for since even after the verb has been parsed no subject information has been introduced into the tree. Since the subject node is not annotated by the information provided by the initial unfixed node (which was instead associated with the object position where it merged), an overt subject NP which appears after the verb phrase is necessary. Again, the close morphological connection (as indicated by the agreement) and prosodic connection (as indicated by the absence of a prosodic break between the verb and the post-verbal NP) reflect the obligatory continuation of the parse and distinguish such clauses from 'after-thought' constructions.

Marten & Gibson (2016) then go on to examine whether the same analysis can be extended to all types of inversion constructions attested in their study. The argument is that the analysis discussed above can also apply to locative inversion and semantic locative inversion. In all these cases, the assumption is that the initial expression does not annotate the logical subject node, but ultimately annotates a node which is only introduced once the verb is parsed (Marten & Gibson 2016).

Another feature of inversion constructions in Bantu languages is that they are not available for object marking. This property can be accounted for naturally under this approach on the basis of the observation that since there is already a locally unfixed node present in the tree following the parse of the subject marker and the tense-aspect marker, it would not be possible for another locally unfixed node (onto which the object marker could be projected) to be introduced into the tree building process. Therefore, the uniform analysis presented is supported by the morphosyntactic and interpretational similarities shared by the inversion constructions examined.

4.5.2. *Bantu passive constructions*

It has also previously been noted that there are similarities between inversion constructions and passive in a number of Bantu languages (Marten & van der Wal 2015; Marten & Gibson 2016). Specifically, in both construction types: (i) the preverbal phrase expresses a role other than the logical subject; (ii) object marking is typically disallowed (although there are exceptions to this generalisation); and (iii) the preverbal phrase is often topical and the postverbal NP (when present) is often focal. Following on from previous accounts of passives as articulated from the DS perspective (Cann 2011; Wu 2011), the account of Bantu passives hinges on the assumption that the initial nominal phrase annotates a LINK structure (or an unfixed node) and that parsing the subject marker licenses the construction of a locally unfixed node. This locally unfixed node is subsequently merged in object position once the verb is parsed. These stages are common to both the inversion structures discussed above and accounts of passives. However, following the parse of the verb in passive constructions there is typically an overt passive marker, such as the passive marker *-w-* found in Swahili.

(66) Kikombe   ki-me-vunj-w-a
       7-cup   SM7-PERF-break-PASS-FV
       'The cup has been broken' (Swahili)

(67) n-á-sít-iré   kʋ-lool-w-a   ní
       SM1sg-PAST1-refuse-PAST1   INF-marry-PASS-FV CONN
       mʋ-keva
       1-poor.person
       'I refused to be married to a poor person' (Rangi, Gibson 2012: 79)

(68) nijó   nyʋʋmbá y-a-táás-irwe
       9.yesterday 9.house   SM9-PAST1-plaster-PERF.PASS
       'Yesterday the house was plastered' (Rangi, Stegen 2002: 13)

The analysis proposed is that the subject annotation is provided by the passive marker. One of the main differences between inversion constructions and passive constructions is that the post-verbal argument is obligatory in the former and optional in the latter. In many instances it is not necessary to include a post-verbal argument (i.e. the agent expression) in passive constructions. The proposal is therefore that due to the presence of the passive marker (which licenses the annotation of the subject node), no postverbal agent needs to be expressed in passive constructions.

(69) Parsing: *Kikombe ki-me-vunj-w-a...*

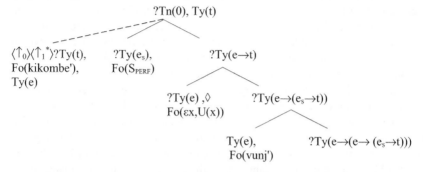

As can be seen in the tree above, the subject node is annotated with a metavariable placeholder (εx, $U(x)$) which can be enriched through the semantics of the predicate (e.g. in the case of *-vunja* 'break' it can be enriched as 'breaker'). When relevant, this can also be further specified by lexical information provided by the optional by-phrase, which is analysed as being projected onto a parallel tree, connected to the main tree via a LINK structure, in line with the analysis presented by Cann (2011: 298). Under this approach, the passive marker, which is parsed after the predicate node has been annotated by the information provided by the verb stem, is modelled as being responsible for the introduction of a pronominal metavariable annotation (representative of semantic underspecification) and the movement of the pointer to the object node. The lexical information which is made available by the parse of the passive marker provides an annotation for the subject node. The remaining outstanding requirement – the ?Ty(e) on the subject node – can be satisfied and the information can be compiled up the tree as the parse is completed.

In this way, the account proposed by Marten & Gibson (2016) for passive constructions in Bantu employs a mechanism of structural underspecification – in the form of the unfixed node onto which the pre-verbal nominal expression is projected (the promoted logical subject). However, in addition to this, the passive marker introduces a metavariable ($\varepsilon x, U(x)$) into the tree which is enriched through the semantics of the predicate (i.e., 'breaker' in the example above). However, this analysis of Bantu passive constructions leaves a number of challenges outstanding. The similarities in the approach for modelling passive constructions and inversion structures were motivated by the observed similarities of these structures. However, as noted above, there are Bantu languages in which object marking is possible in passive constructions (although this is not true of inversion constructions). The issue of whether this approach can therefore be extended to languages in which object marking is allowed in passives is therefore one issue to consider in further detail. In a similar vein, if such an extension to languages in which object marking is permitted in passives is possible, this raises additional challenges for the current approach, which in many ways hinges on the use of the locally unfixed node for the processing of the pre-verbal argument. Similarly, the pointer movement induced by parsing the passive marker is a crucial element of this account. But if an intervening element (i.e. an object marker) is present in the verb structure, this would render the current analysis untenable and necessitate an alternate analysis, since it would result in the introduction of 'second' locally unfixed node with a distinct annotation, in contradiction of the tree node logic.

Marten & Gibson (2016) are very clear about these potential issues with their analyses, and these challenges will not be resolved in the current discussion. However, what can be said here is that a potential analysis within the DS framework may involve the exploration of a more fine-grained typology of Bantu object markers, in line with the proposals made by Woolford (1995) and Zeller (2012). In some Bantu languages, object markers could be considered to decorate a LINK structure. Alternatively, an approach in which a complex of unfixed nodes is dominated by a single unfixed node relation could be pursued (as will also be seen in relation to multiple object markers in Section 3.5). This would therefore have the desired effect of avoiding the co-occurrence of multiple object markers. An alternative approach may also involve the notion of the anticipation of the (eventual) passive marker, in line with the approach taken to modelling tense-aspect-mood suffixes.

4.6. SUMMARY

This chapter has provided a snapshot of the way in which the notions of underspecification and update are manifested across the Bantu clause. Under-specification can be seen to be central in the DS approach where the manipulation of information at any and every given stage of the tree building process plays a crucial role in the establishment of propositional structure. As was seen in this chapter, both structural underspecification – in the form of unfixed nodes – and semantic underspecification – captured primarily by recourse to metavariable placeholders – are heavily involved in the unfolding of tree structure for the modelling of clauses in Bantu languages. This chapter has shown underspecfication in terms of the verb stem itself, as well as underspecified temporal relations in the account of Bantu tense-aspect prefixes and suffixes.

Whilst this chapter has presented a number of case studies and highlighted the role of underspecification, the effects of these formal mechanisms can be seen across a wide range of phenomena and will be seen throughout this study. This includes the discussion of negation (particularly in relation to negative copula constructions) in Chapter 5, which will be seen to rely on the use of a metavariable placeholder to account for negation. Similarly, Chapter 6 which examines auxiliary constructions will be seen to rely on the notion that structure, once introduced, can be re-built over and over again, as long as the information which annotates the nodes is compatible.

Whilst DS assumes that elements are associated with their own lexically-specified contribution to the tree building process, lexical items do not make a single fixed set of syntactic and/or semantic contributions to the clause in which they appear, rather the actions induced are inherently related to the context. The contribution made to the parse and the associated unfolding of the trees, can therefore be considered to be dependent on the tree state that holds at the point at which they are encountered, as well as the other elements which are present in the tree at that point. In this way, underspecification can also be used to capture the expectation for a particular type of information, even if it has not yet been introduced into the tree (as in a requirement for a copy in the case of a LINK structure or an enrichment of a metavariable). Alternatively, it can be used to represent a partially fulfilled annotation in a tree, such as an unfixed tree node address. Unfixed tree node addresses contain some information about the position of the node within the tree, but this information is not sufficient to enable the establishment of a fixed tree node address. Finally, a further assumption made by the DS approach is that the concepts of underspecification and attendant update are not merely a property of some semantic or pragmatic sub-system, or of an independently defined parser but are rather considered to be an inherent part of the syntactic mechanism.

5

MODELLING NEGATION IN BANTU:
THE DYNAMICS OF INTERPRETATION

This chapter explores the issues and challenges raised by negative constructions for a Dynamic Syntax account of Bantu clause structure. Across the Bantu language family, a wide range of strategies are used for the encoding of negation, including the presence of segmental morphological markers, dedicated tonal patterns, auxiliaries and independent particles. Whilst some languages make recourse to only one of these means for encoding negation, other languages use two or more strategies. Another widely attested distributional pattern found across Bantu includes variation in negation strategies according to specific tense-aspect combinations, as well as sensitivity to main clause versus non-main clause conditions.

A fully-specified account of negation within Dynamic Syntax remains to be developed and this chapter alone will not be able to address this gap in the framework. However, the chapter takes common negation strategies found in the Bantu languages as a starting point for exploring the issues involved in representing negation from a DS perspective. The chapter focuses on the contribution made to the tree building process by segmental markers of negation. The contribution to the tree logic as conveyed by independent negative markers, as well as negative copulas is also examined.

Morphological markers of negation commonly interact with temporal and aspectual information, and the account developed here will reflect this observation. Morphological negative markers will be shown to not only contribute negative polarity to the clause, but also to induce the building of fixed tree structure, reflective of their interaction with the broader tense-aspect system. In contrast, independent negative markers will be shown not to contribute to the tree building process apart from the introduction of the information encoding negative polarity. Finally, negative copula forms will be shown to be the most underspecified in terms of content but to make the most substantial contribution to the tree building process through the introduction of fixed predicate-argument structure in addition to the situation argument node for the hosting of temporal and aspectual information, as well as indicating the negative polarity status of the clause.

The chapter draws on data from Swahili and Rangi, showing the way in which distinct accounts are necessary in order to capture the differences between the two languages, whilst also being underpinned by recourse to the same formal strategies and the associated structures. The chapter concludes with a discussion of the questions raised in developing an account of the diachronic development of negation strategies attested in Bantu, setting an agenda for possible avenues of future research.

5.1. Previous accounts of negation in DS

A number of previous studies articulated within the DS approach have sought to examine negation either as the primary focus, for example, the account of negative indefinites in Maltese by of Lucas (2014) or as part of a broader exploration of issues in which negation plays a role, as in the case of clitic placement in Romance and varieties of Modern Greek in Bouzouita (2008a; 2008b) and Chatzikyriakidis (2010) respectively. Also included in this latter category is the study contained in Gibson (2012) which examines auxiliary placement in Rangi where negation is one of the contexts which triggers auxiliary-verb order (as discussed in further detail below). This section provides a summary of the previous accounts of negation which have been developed from the perspective of the DS approach. In doing so, it lays the foundation for the account of negation in Swahili and Rangi which constitute Section 5.3 and Section 5.4 below.

Bouzouita (2008b) examines the diachronic development of the Spanish clitic system. In Medieval Spanish, clitics can appear adjoined either before the verb (as proclitics) or after the verb (as enclitics). Part of what determines the position in which the clitic appears is the syntactic environment in which they are found. One of the environments in which proclisis is found is with negative clauses. The analysis developed for clitics in Medieval Spanish are also examined in Chapter 7 where the cross-linguistic parallels between a number of phenomena are discussed. However, for the current discussion it is sufficient to focus on the method of representation employed to capture negation.

In Medieval Spanish, negative adverbs such as *no(n)* 'not' and *nunca/nunqua* 'never', as well as negative coordination involving the conjunction *ni(n)* 'neither/nor' are associated with preverbal clitics in negative finite contexts. To account for proclisis in negative environments, Bouzouita (2008b) makes recourse to the negative feature [+NEG]. This negative feature is part of the complex lexical entry for the clitic *lo*, where it is one of three lexical triggers which enables the parsing of the clitic.

(70) Lexical for the Medieval Spanish clitic *lo* (Bouzouita 2008b: 303)

IF	?Ty(t)		
THEN	IF	$[NEG+] \lor$	} Negative marker
		$(\langle\downarrow*\rangle Fo(\alpha), ?\exists x.Tn(x)) \lor$	} Unfixed node
		$?\exists x.Tns(x)$	} Tense requirement
	THEN	$make(\langle\downarrow_1\rangle); go(\langle\downarrow_1\rangle);$	
		$make(\langle\downarrow_0\rangle); go(\langle\downarrow_0\rangle);$	
		$put(U, Ty(e), ?\exists x.Fo(x),$	
		$[\downarrow]\bot, ?\langle\uparrow_0\rangle Ty(e\rightarrow t))$	
	ELSE	abort	

ELSE   IF $?Ty(e),\langle\uparrow\rangle T$
    THEN   IF $\langle\uparrow_0\uparrow_1{}^*\rangle$ $(?Ty(t), [NEG+], ?\exists x.Tns(x)) \vee$
                    $\langle\uparrow_0\uparrow_1{}^*\rangle$ $(?Ty(t), \langle\downarrow*\rangle$ $(Fo(\alpha), ?\exists x.Tn(x)),$
                    $\exists x.Tns(x)) \vee$
                    $\langle\uparrow_0\uparrow_1{}^*\rangle^+(?Ty(t), ?\exists x.Tns(x))$
    THEN   abort
    ELSE $put(U, Ty(e), ?\exists x.Fo(x),$
              $[\downarrow]\bot,?\langle\uparrow_0\rangle Ty(e{\rightarrow}t))$
   ELSE   abort

As can be seen on examination of the lexical entry in (70) above, there are two triggers in this lexical characterisation: preverbal clitics are constructed from a type-t-requiring node (as captured by the requirement ?Ty(t)), whilst the type-e-requiring node trigger is used to capture post-verbal clitics. The negative feature [NEG+] is assumed to be projected by the negative marker on the type t-requiring node and signals the presence of a negative operator in the clause. The clitic can be parsed when this [NEG+] feature is present thereby giving rise to proclisis.

The feature [NEG+] is merely a placeholder for a full analysis of negation. However, based on discussion with Ruth Kempson, Bouzouita (2008b: 222ff) notes that an appropriate avenue for a formal analysis of negation may involve positing the projection of a term indicating 'no witness' as a result of parsing a negative element, and that negation could decorate an unfixed node. This would be in line with the account of other quantification and indefinite NPs which are also taken as decorating unfixed nodes. The negative feature will also be used in the working analysis for negation Rangi developed below, whilst the association of negation with an unfixed node will be seen in the account developed for auxiliary constructions in Chapter 6.

Chatzikyriakidis (2010) examines the clitic system of four varieties of Modern Greek. The systems under examination exhibit clitic placement patterns which are determined by the syntactic environment in which they occur and, as the account argues, the processing conditions with which they are associated. Clitics in Cypriot Greek are generally enclitic in both imperative and non-imperative contexts. However, proclisis obtains when one of a variety of functional elements appears at the left periphery: wh-elements, tense and modality markers (including subjunctive markers, negative particles and the future particle) focused constituents and subordinating conjunctions.[22]

The three triggering contexts for Cypriot Greek are summarised in (71) below.[23]

---

[22] A third category in which the placement of the clitic varies involves complements of non-factive verbs introduced with the non-factive complementiser *oti* and subordinates of cause introduced via *epiδi*, *γiati* 'because'. This category is not discussed in any further detail here since it is not relevant for the current discussion.

[23] The vertical line in the lexical entry shown in (72) above indicates an inclusive disjunction, meaning that both triggers are satisfied.

(71) Contexts which trigger proclisis in Cypriot Greek (Chatzikyriakidis
2010: 206)

```
IF      ?Ty(t)
THEN  IF      ⟨↓*⟩?∃x.Tn(x))|
               ⟨↓0⟩?Ty(eₛ)|
               [+NEG]
       THEN
       ELSE  abort
ELSE  abort
```

As can be seen on examination of the partial lexical entry above, the proclisis
contexts are: (i) the presence of an unfixed node; (ii) the presence of a type-e_s-
requiring node; and (iii) the negation trigger.

In the same vein as the approach adopted by Bouzouita (2008b), Chatzikyriakidis (2010) initially develops an account which employs the negative feature
[+NEG]. However, the subsequent discussion proposes that the explicit inclusion
of the negative feature is not necessary. The proposal is that the negative
contexts in which proclisis is triggered can also be captured by employing the
first two parsing contexts: the presence of an unfixed node ($⟨↓*⟩?∃x.Tn(x)$) and
the presence of a type-e_s requiring node ($?Ty(e_s)$). This proposal is based on the
following observation: there are two types of negation in Cypriot Greek – one
used in the indicative and one used in subjunctive and imperative environments.
It is therefore proposed that the patterning restrictions associated with these
forms can be captured on the situation argument node – the locus for the
encoding of tense-aspect information – since negation interacts with tense-
aspect. This information can be encoded inside the complex situation argument
node with negation markers projecting their restrictions inside this node.

A similar analysis is proposed for clitics in Standard Modern Greek (SMG)
and Grecia Salentina Greek (GSG). Imperatives in SMG and GSG cannot be
negated. Chatzikyriakidis (2010) proposes that this observation can be correctly
captured by an analysis under which negation builds the situation argument node
and decorates this node with a type e_s requirement. This is based on the proposal
that parsing negative elements results in the construction of fixed tree structure
and that the trigger which was posited for imperatives – that all nodes must be
unfixed when they come into parse (Chatzikyriakidis 2010: 130) – will not be
satisfied in such an instance. Whilst the analysis does not provide the precise
formal details, this will be seen to have parallels with the account developed
below for modelling negation in Swahili and Rangi.

The account developed for negative concord in Maltese (and negative concord
languages more broadly) by Lucas (2014) hinges on the observation that
negation is a property of sentences (or propositions) rather than of lexical items
per se. In this regard, the approach is able to capture the difference in behaviour
between negative words in Standard English and n-words in negative concord
languages such as Maltese.

The essence of the analysis is that negative expressions such as *no one* and *nothing* always automatically decorate the Ty(t) root node with a negative polarity feature (Pol(NEG)) whenever they are encountered. In contrast, n-words, such as *xejn* in Maltese, are sensitive to whether the Ty(t) node already has this negative polarity decoration or not. Whilst the additional details of the account are beyond the scope of the current discussion, Lucas (2014), in common with the account proposed by Chatzikyriakidis (2010), also suggests that a future account of negation from the DS perspective may employ the situation argument node.

It is important to note that the annotation Pol(NEG) is a diacritic in DS and serves merely to stand in until a fully specified account of negation has been developed in the framework. There is, in principle, no limit on the number of possible labels of this type that can be employed, and as the framework continues to develop and accounts are formulated for a wider range of phenomena and languages it may well be necessary to employ similar labels until fully-specified analyses are developed. It is also possible for certain annotations to be comprised of other parts. Recourse has been made previously to at least Pol(Neg), Force(COND) for conditional clauses and Force(INT) for interrogative clauses. However, a general guiding principle is to aim to reduce and ultimately eliminate these diacritic annotations, replacing them with specific analyses that derive from the incremental growth of propositional structure.

For the purposes of the current discussion, the simplified means of representing negation will continue to be used and negative polarity is indicated as a feature with the value Pol(Neg). In theory, affirmative propositions can also be indicated through the use of the diacritic Pol(Aff) however, by being unmarked, propositions are assumed to be affirmative. A snapshot of the tree representing a basic negative sentence such as the English phrase *Clayton does not like Musa*, employing the negative polarity diacritic Pol(Neg) is shown in (72) below.

(72)   Final tree state for *Clayton does not like Musa*

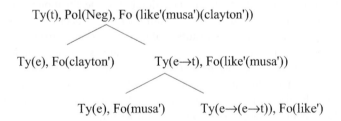

The account developed in Gibson (2012) employed the negative feature [+ NEG]. The annotation Cat(Neg) at the root node was assumed to be introduced by the negation marker. The annotation Cat(Neg) is similar to Pol (Neg) but it employs Polarity rather than Category, the latter of which could refer to a much broader category of information. The use of the negative feature

[+ NEG] and the negative diacritic at the root node followed the work of Bouzouita (2008a; 2008b) and Chatzikyriakidis (2010) as discussed above. Since the focus of Gibson (2012) was on auxiliary placement in Rangi, negation was only examined to the extent that it played a role in these constructions. Negation in Rangi auxiliary constructions is formed through a bipartite construction in which the negative copula appears before the verbal complex and the negative marker *tʋkʋ* appears after this form. The analysis further proposed that this first negative marker was projected onto an unfixed predicate node, thereby enabling the auxiliary to be parsed as the next item in the clause and accounting for the auxiliary-verb order. This analysis was consistent with the proposal of an unfixed node as a generalised trigger across all of the contexts in which auxiliary-verb order was found in compound constructions. No further details of this account will be presented here since general sentential negation and negative copulas in Rangi are discussed in Section 5.4 below and auxiliary constructions (including those associated with negation) are discussed in Chapter 6.

5.2. NEGATION IN BANTU

Bantu languages employ a wide range of strategies for encoding negation. The use of negative affixes, auxiliary-based constructions, independent words, or combination of these strategies are common methods across the language family. The number and location in which negation is indicated varies between languages, with single, double and triple marking attested, as well as different positions within the verb and/or clause being available for marking negation. Variation in Bantu negation strategies has been the subject of a number of previous studies (e.g. Kamba Muzenga 1981; Güldemann 1996; 1999; Devos & van der Auwera 2013; Gibson & Guérois 2017).

A common strategy for indicating negation amongst the Bantu languages is the use of morphological markers which appear as part of the Bantu verb form (cf. Meeussen 1967; Kamba Muzenga 1981). Two positions are frequently employed for the marking of negation within the verbal template: the pre-initial position (i.e. before the subject marker) and the post-initial position (i.e. after the subject marker). Historically, these two positions reflect a distinction between clause types, with pre-initial negation commonly associated with main clauses and post-initial negation associated with non-main clause contexts such as infinitives, relatives and subjunctives (Güldemann 1996; 1999). This is a distinction which has been retained in many Bantu languages.

Present tense negation in Swahili is marked through the presence of a negative subject marker and the final vowel appearing as -*i* (instead of the final vowel -*a* which appears in indicative contexts).[24] An additional difference between the

---

[24] An exception to this is if the verb already ends in either -*u* or -*i* (which are historically verbs of Arabic origin) in which case no change takes place.

negative and affirmative verb forms in the present tense in Swahili is that there is no overt morphological marking of tense in the negative present. This can be seen on comparison of the examples below where the sentence in (73) shows an affirmative present tense sentence, whilst (74) shows a negative present tense example. As noted above, another common feature of negation in Bantu is a distinction between negation strategies in main clause and dependent clause contexts. This pattern is also reflected in Swahili, where negation is marked in the post-initial position in the negative subjunctive (75).

(73) Tu-na-pik-a   wali
      SM1pl-CONT-cook-FV   rice
      'we are cooking rice' (Swahili)

(74) Hatu-pik-i   wali
      NEG.SM1pl-cook-FV   rice
      'we are not cooking rice' (Swahili)

(75) U-si-end-e!
      SM2-NEG-go-SBJV
      'don't go!' (Swahili)

The form involved in negative constructions in Swahili varies across tenses. Whilst the present tense negative is unmarked for tense, in the past tense the marker *ku-* appears before the verb stem and the final vowel remains as -*a*. Future tense negation shows yet a different strategy at play with the negative subject marker employed alongside the future tense prefix *ta-* and the final vowel appearing as -*a*.

There is also variation in the way negation is encoded between the Bantu languages. Negation can be indicated through the presence of a single marker in the clause, as is seen in Swahili. Alternatively, negation can be marked more than once within a clause. Lubukusu and Kuria both exhibit double negation through the combination of a pre-initial negative marker and a post-verbal independent negative marker in the clause, as in examples (76) and (77) below.

(76) Wakesa **se**-a-a-tim-a   **ta**
      Wakesa NEG-1SM-PST-run-FV   NEG
      'Wekesa did not run' (Lubukusu, Wasike 2007: 243)

(77) **Te**-bá-som-ere   **hai**
      NEG-SM2-read-PFV   NEG
      'they have not read today' (Kuria, Cammenga 2004)

In some languages, negation is marked outside of the verb form, as is the case in Tumbuka where negation is indicated through an independent negative particle – *yayi*, as can be seen in example (78).

(78) Msambizgi wa-ku-timb-a   wana   **yayi** lero
    1.teacher   sm1-pres-hit-fv 2.child   neg   nowadays
    'the teacher does not hit children these days' (Tumbuka, Chavula 2016)

In Salampasu, negation is marked in three locations within the clause: through the presence of a pre-initial and a post-stem marker on the inflected verb form, as well as an independent negative particle which appears clause-finally (79).

(79) **káá**-dédélo-**kú**   mu-tóndú **ba**
    neg1-cut.pfv-neg   3-tree   neg
    'he hasn't cut a tree.' (Salampasu, Ngalamulume 1977, cited in Devos & van der Auwera 2013: 210)

Having provided a brief overview of the strategies employed for marking negation that are seen across Bantu, this chapter explores the issues involved in the development of an account of negation in Bantu from the perspective of Dynamic Syntax. The chapter draws on data from Swahili and Rangi and focuses on the contribution of dedicated negative segmental morphology and independent negative markers to the structure building process. Whilst the chapter will present only detailed accounts of negation in these two languages, it is proposed that in many instances similar principles can be extended to negation in other Bantu languages, since the analyses rely on the central concepts of underspecification, incremental update and the contribution made by the negative elements in a clause.

5.3. Modelling negation in Swahili

5.3.1. *Sentential negation in Swahili main clauses*

The primary challenges involved in modelling negation in Swahili from a Dynamic Syntax perspective relate to the contribution of the negative markers to the propositional structure, and in ensuring that the interaction between the tense-aspect information, the subject information and the negative polarity of the sentence is accurately represented. It is also crucial to capture the restrictions relating to the ordering of the morphemes within the verbal template, as well as more broadly across the clause.

The assumption made here is that the same broad steps are employed for parsing a Swahili negative sentence as those presented in Chapter 2 for modelling Swahili affirmative clauses. Specifically, a potential subject expression (when present) is projected onto a partial tree connected to the main tree via a link relation that is established following the application of the rule of link adjunction. The various elements that comprise the inflected verb form subsequently make their own lexically-specified contribution to the tree-building process, resulting in the unfolding of propositional structure as the subject marker, tense-aspect marker(s) and verb stem are parsed. However, in negative sentences in Swahili, the negative polarity of the clause is also marked in at least one instance within the verb. This section will present an account of main clause negation in Swahili, whilst an exploration of the potential for this account to be extended to dependent clauses is presented in Section 5.3.2.

Consider the sentences below. Whilst example (80) shows a negative present tense form, the example in (81) shows the future tense negative and (82) shows the past tense negative form.

(80) Ha-pik-i   wali na   ma-harage
      NEG.SM1-cook-FV rice CONN 6-beans
      's/he is not cooking rice and beans' (Swahili)

(81) Hatu-ta-som-a   ki-tabu hiki
      NEG.SM1pl-FUT-read-FV   7-book   7.DEM
      'we will not read this book.' (Swahili)

(82) Ha-ku-fik-a   shule-ni
      NEG.SM1-PAST-arrive-FV   9.school-LOC
      's/he did not arrive at school.' (Swahili)

The first element to be parsed in these sentences is the negative subject marker. Parsing the class 1 negative subject marker *ha-* results in the projection of this information onto a locally unfixed node introduced by the rule of LOCAL *ADJUNCTION. Negative subject markers also annotate this locally unfixed node with a metavariable which restricts the possible interpretation of the referent to the noun class in question, as determined by the class information encoded by the subject marker. In the case of *ha-*, this introduces a class 1 restriction into the tree, meaning that the ultimate interpretation of this metavariable must be compatible with class 1 semantics. Both in terms of the projection of a locally unfixed node and the introduction of a metavariable annotation, the analysis of the negative subject marker is the same as that proposed for the affirmative subject marker (see Section 3.2). However, since *ha-* is inherently negative, it is also proposed that this marker introduces the negative polarity information into the clause – represented by the *pro tem* annotation Pol(Neg) at the root node.[25]

The negative subject marker is also considered to be responsible for the construction of the situation argument node. This reflects the close relationship between tense-aspect marking and negation in Bantu (see also the discussion in Chatzikyriakidis 2010: 207 for a similar observation for varieties of Greek). Such a proposal is also necessary to be able to account for the absence of any overt morphological marking of tense in the present tense negative verb form in Swahili.

[25] In Swahili, the prefix *ha-* encodes both negative polarity and class 1 subject information. This is also the case for the first person singular negative marker *si-* which is also only mono-morphemic. For other person/number or class information, it can be assumed that the negative marker introduces the negative polarity and that the subject marker encodes the subject information.

Recall that, in the analysis presented so far, it has been the pre-stem marker which is responsible for the introduction of the situation argument node and the predicate-requiring node which provides the triggering conditions that enable the verb stem to be parsed. Analysing the negative subject marker as projecting a situation argument node and fixed minimal predicate structure, thus enables the development of a uniform analysis of main clause affirmative and negative clauses in terms of structure building, and particularly the contribution of the verb stem to this process. The proposed lexical entry for the negative subject marker *ha-* is shown in (83) below.

(83) Lexical entry for the Swahili negative subject marker *ha-*

> *Ha-* IF $?Ty(e), \langle\uparrow_0\rangle\langle\uparrow_1{*}\rangle?Ty(t)$
> THEN $put(Ty(e), Fo(U_{CLASS1}), ?\exists x.Fo(x)); go(\langle\uparrow_0\rangle\langle\uparrow_1{*}\rangle),$
> $put(Pol(Neg)), make(\langle\downarrow_0\rangle); go(\langle\downarrow_0\rangle); put(Ty(e_s) go(\langle\uparrow_0\rangle);$
> $make(\langle\downarrow_1\rangle); go(\langle\downarrow_1\rangle); put(?Ty(e_s \to t)); make(\langle\downarrow_1\rangle);$
> $go(\langle\downarrow_1\rangle); put(?Ty(e \to (e_s \to t)));$
> ELSE   abort

Parsing negative subject markers is therefore considered to result in the unfolding of more extensive tree structure than their affirmative counterparts. Whilst affirmative subject markers are also projected onto a locally unfixed node, they provide only an annotation for this node, whilst negative subject markers also introduce the situation argument node and provide the annotation of the root node with negative polarity. This more extensive structure building is justified in the case of negative subject markers since the conditions in which these steps unfold are highly constrained – i.e. they only occur in contexts in which negative subject markers are present.

(84) Parsing: *Ha-*

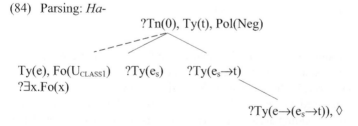

$?Tn(0), Ty(t), Pol(Neg)$

$Ty(e), Fo(U_{CLASS1})$ $?Ty(e_s)$ $?Ty(e_s \to t)$
$?\exists x.Fo(x)$

                                        $?Ty(e \to (e_s \to t)), \lozenge$

In a present tense negative verb form, the next element to be encountered after the subject marker is the verb stem. Recall that the triggering conditions for parsing the verb stem is the presence of the $?Ty(e \to (e_s \to t))$ node. The lexical entry for *-pik* 'cook' is shown in (85) below.

(85) Lexical entry for the verb stem *-pik-* 'cook'

-*pik-* IF $?Ty(e \rightarrow (e_s \rightarrow t))$
         THEN $go(\langle \uparrow_1 \rangle)$; $make(\langle \downarrow_0 \rangle)$; $go(\langle \downarrow_0 \rangle)$; $put(?Ty(e)))$; $go(\langle \uparrow_0 \rangle)$;
                $make(\langle \downarrow_1 \rangle)$; $go(\langle \downarrow_1 \rangle)$; $make(\langle \downarrow_0 \rangle)$; $go(\langle \downarrow_0 \rangle)$; $put(?Ty(e))$;
                $go(\langle \uparrow_0 \rangle)$; $make(\langle \downarrow_1 \rangle)$; $go(\langle \downarrow_1 \rangle)$; $put(Fo(pik')$,
                $Ty(e \rightarrow (e \rightarrow (e_s \rightarrow))))$; $go(\langle \uparrow_1 \rangle)$
         ELSE   abort

When these conditions are met, the verb stem can be parsed, resulting in the introduction of additional predicate-argument structure as determined by the valency of the verb stem (in line with the account forwarded by Marten 2002). Any potential subject information can provide interpretation for the subject node and the predicate node is annotated by the lexico-semantic information provided by the verb stem. The emerging tree state is shown in (86) below where the class 1 referent *Mwaasʊ* (a person's name) has been substituted as the subject argument.

(86) Parsing: *ha-pik-i…* 's/he is not cooking…'

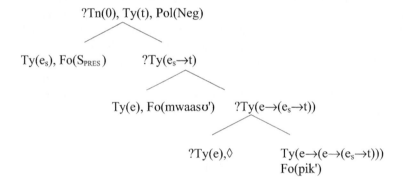

Under this account, the final vowel -*i* involved in the negative present tense is analysed as not introducing any new structure into the tree or making a semantic contribution to the tree. Rather, it is modelled in the same way as the default final vowel -*a* was analysed in Section 3.6 – as responsible for movement of the pointer to the corresponding argument node. In the case of a transitive predicate, this will result in the movement of the pointer to the object node. Indeed, this is what is seen in the current example, with the pointer at the object node, the expression *wali* 'rice' can be parsed. The information is compiled up the tree and with all of the requirements satisfied, the parse is complete. A snapshot of the final tree state is shown in (87).

(87) Parsing: *Hapiki wali* 's/he is not cooking rice'

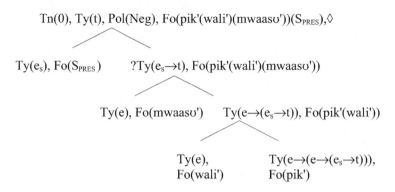

In this analysis, no specific mention is made of the tense information. The assumption here is that although there is no overt pre-stem tense marker in the present tense negative form, it is the very absence of this marker which results in the present tense reading. This analysis is possible since the present tense is the only negative form in which there is no pre-stem marker – recall that both the past and future tense negative forms have an overt tense marker. The proposal is therefore that if the negative subject marker is followed by the future tense marker *ta-* or by the negative past tense marker *ku-* then these temporal readings will be introduced into the tree and annotate the situation argument node. However, the absence of a pre-stem tense-aspect marker results in the default present tense interpretation.

Parsing negative future tense and negative past tense verb forms would involve a similar unfolding of the tree, with the negative subject marker projected onto a locally unfixed node and inducing a situation argument node and the negative polarity annotation on the root node. In (81) the subsequent parsing of the future tense marker *ta-* would result in the introduction of the future tense information to the situation argument node, whilst in example (82), parsing *ku-* induces the past tense annotation. In both cases, the remainder of the clause is parsed following the steps set out above, with the verb introducing fixed structure and the corresponding lexical semantics into the clause. In the negative present tense, where there is no overt morphological marking of tense, the tense interpretation is the result of a default reading, and the present tense information annotates the situation argument node.

5.3.2. *Negation in Swahili non-main clause contexts*

The account above can be used to model negation in Swahili main clause contexts where negation is marked through the presence of a pre-initial negative. This reflects the dominant historical pattern for encoding negation in Bantu main clauses which is more commonly associated with the pre-initial position. However, as was noted above, non-main clause contexts commonly employ the

post-initial position for marking negation (Güldemann 1996; 1999). This is also
the pattern that is observed in Swahili. Negative imperatives in Swahili for
example, employ the same subject markers as the affirmative verb forms, but
with the addition of the negative marker *si-* which appears after the subject
marker. This post-initial negative marker *si-* is invariable and remains the same
across all noun classes and person/number distinctions. Similarly, in the negative
subjunctive, the verb form employs the same subject marker forms as were seen
in the affirmative but with the addition of the post-initial position negative
marker *si-*. The negative subjunctive is used when the subject of the main verb
and its complement are different, as in example (88). The construction is
identical to the negative imperative however, which can be seen in example (89).

(88) A-li-ni-ambi-a   ni-si-pik-e   cha-kula
      SM1-PAST-OM1sg-tell-FV SM1sg-NEG-cook-SBJV 7-food
      's/he told me not to cook' (Swahili)

(89) U-si-end-e!
      SM2-NEG-go-SBJV
      'don't go!' (Swahili)

Since the linear order of words and morphemes is central to the DS approach, the
first element parsed in a sentence such as that shown in example (89) is the
subject marker. The subject marker is projected onto a locally unfixed node
introduced by the rule of LOCAL *ADJUNCTION. The next element to be parsed is the
post-initial negative marker *si-*. The presence of the locally unfixed node is
considered to provide the requisite triggering conditions for the negative marker
si- to be parsed. The negative marker introduces the negative polarity value to
the clause, as well as the situation argument node (as was also seen with the pre-
initial negative subject markers). With the necessary conditions present in the
tree, the verb stem can then be parsed.

The Swahili negative imperative verb form is also associated with the presence
of the final vowel -*e*. Parsing -*e* serves to introduce the subjunctive mood into the
clause. This is represented by the annotation Mood (subjunctive) on the situation
argument. This follows the analysis proposed by Chatzikyriakidis (2010: 30) for
Salentina Modern Greek and Grecia Salentina Greek under which the annotation
(mood (x)) was introduced on the situation argument node, where mood is seen
as a predicate where x ranges over a set of possible mood values. A similar
proposal is extended to those constructions in Swahili in which the subjunctive
form is used when a verb with a different subject appears in the subjunctive form
as the complement of a main verb, as in example (88) above. Whilst such an
analysis can capture the facts of the subjunctive verb form, overall, these
constructions would be modelled by recourse to a bi-clausal analysis, which
would employ two trees constructed in parallel and connected via a LINK relation.

5.4. MODELLING NEGATION IN RANGI

5.4.1. *Rangi main clause negation*

Negation in Rangi is encoded through the presence of a segmental morphological marker of negation. In contrast to negation in Swahili, in Rangi main clauses the negative marker is invariable and does not interact with the subject marking of the clause. The pre-verbal negative marker consistently appears as *sí*. In addition to the marker *sí*, Rangi also employs the independent negative particle *toko* which is obligatory in declarative main clauses (91). The marker *toko* can appear either post-verbally or clause-finally (92).

(90) Sí   n-íyó-dóm-a   toko
     NEG SM1sg-PROG-go-FV NEG
     'I am not going'

(91) *Sí   n-íyó-dom-a   na   Dodoma
      NEG SM1sg-PROG-go-FV CONN Dodoma
     'I am not going to Dodoma'

(92) Mo-sungaati sí   a-lóng-aa   na   mo-keva
     1-rich.person NEG SM1.PRES-spend.day-PRES.HAB CONN 1-poor.person
     toko
     NEG
     'a rich person does not spend the day with a poor person'

The fact that negation in Rangi employs an invariable negation marker which does not interact with the subject marker necessitates a slightly different analysis from that developed above for Swahili.

Following on from the account presented in Section 5.3 for Swahili, verbal negation in Rangi is also modelled by recourse to the introduction of negative polarity information which appears at the root node. The proposal here is that the Rangi negative marker *sí* introduces the requirement for the negative polarity annotation (?Pol(Neg)) into the tree. In order for the parse to be successful, this negative requirement must be satisfied before the end of the parse. However, the marker *sí* is not considered to be responsible for the introduction of this feature. Rather this feature is only satisfied following the parse of the post-verbal negative marker *toko*, reflecting its obligatory status within the clause.[26]

As can be seen on examination of the lexical entry below, the negative marker *sí* introduces the negative polarity requirement ?Pol(Neg) into the tree as an

---

[26] A similar proposal in which one (type of) negative marker introduces a requirement for negative polarity and a second negative marker or negative word is required to satisfy this requirement is proposed by Lucas (2014) for Maltese.

annotation at the root node. The marker is not analysed as making any other contribution to the tree, though its lexical entry will be examined in more detail below (and in Chapter 6).

(93) Lexical entry for the Rangi negative marker *sí*

    sí IF   ?Ty(t),
         THEN put(?Pol(Neg))
             . . .
         ELSE abort

The main verb is then parsed in the way outlined in Chapter 3, with the subject marker being projected onto a locally unfixed node, the tense-aspect marker introducing a situation argument node and fixed structure before the verb stem being parsed. After the other elements in the clause, the negative marker *toko* is then encountered. It is proposed here that it is this marker which is responsible for the introduction of the negative polarity annotation at the root node, satisfying the requirement ?Pol(Neg). However, *toko* does not make any contribution to the tree building process or to structural relations, but merely satisfies the requirement for negative polarity. A snapshot of the final tree is shown in (94) below where an appropriate substituent for the first person singular (i.e. speaker) is provided from context by *Mwaasʋ*.

(94) Parsing: *Sí níyódóma toko* 'I am not going'

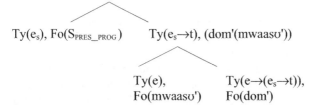

$Tn(0), Ty(t), Fo(dom'(mwaasʋ')), Pol(Neg) (S_{PRES\_PROG}), \Diamond$

$Ty(e_s), Fo(S_{PRES\_PROG})$ $Ty(e_s{\rightarrow}t), (dom'(mwaasʋ'))$

         $Ty(e),$ $Ty(e{\rightarrow}(e_s{\rightarrow}t)),$
         $Fo(mwaasʋ')$ $Fo(dom')$

5.4.2. *Rangi non-main clause negation*

Whilst negation in declarative main clause negation is achieved through the combination of *sí* and *toko*, there are two non-main clause constructions in which the negative marker *toko* is used without *sí*. These contexts are the prohibitive (95) and the negative infinitive (96).

(95) ku-n-va-a   na   nkome toko!
     INF-OM1sg-hit-FV CONN 9.stick NEG
     'do not hit me with a stick!' (Rangi, Dunham 1996–2004 corpus:
     Hyena and hare)

(96) ...na pat-a   tʊkʊ mpaka kw-a   kw-iir-a.
CONN get-FV NEG   until   15-of INF-get.dark-FV
'... and not catching anything until nightfall' (Rangi, Stegen 2011: 163)

The claim here is that the analysis developed above for the bipartite negation construction in Rangi can be naturally extended to capture the constructions in which *tʊkʊ* alone is used to encoded negation. The marker *sí* only introduces a requirement for negative polarity and must therefore be followed by a negative polarity encoding element (such as *tʊkʊ*) in order for the sentence to be felicitous. However, this is not true for *tʊkʊ* which introduces the negative polarity independently of the preceding structure and whether any negative information has already been introduced into the tree at the point when it is parsed.

This approach can therefore account for the grammaticality of the prohibitive sentence in (95) above, as well as its negative polarity. The parse proceeds in the same manner as for an affirmative clause until *tʊkʊ* is encountered. The word does not contribute to the tree building structure but merely introduces the negative polarity information (represented by Pol(Neg)) into the tree. The same analysis can be extended to the negative infinitive construction, which in (96) is formed in much the same way as the prohibitive, with the negative marker *tʊkʊ* appearing after the infinitival verb form and providing only the annotation for the root node.

This account can also be extended to negative possessive constructions which are formed in Rangi using either the form *-sina* 'not have' or the form *-tʊte* 'have' which can be prefixed by negative subject information.[27]

(97) mpichi i-sina   mʊ-ryoongo   tʊkʊ
9.hyena SM9.NEG.have 3-brain   NEG
'the hyena has no brains' (Rangi, Dunham 1996–2004 corpus: *Hyena and hare*)

(98) nɪ́ɪni   sin-tʊte   ki-taabu tʊkʊ
1sg.PP SM.NEG1sg-have 7-book   NEG
'I do not have a book' (Rangi, Gibson 2012: 100)

Another instance in which the negative marker appears in the post-initial position is in negative subjunctive clauses. This can be seen in example (99) which also shows the formation of the negative conditional where, although *sí* appears after the conditional marker *ka-*, can still be considered to occupy the pre-initial position since it appears before the first person plural subject marker *t-*

---

[27] The form *-sina* 'not be, not have' appears to be (at least historically) derived from a combination of the negative marker *si-* and the commitative *na* 'and, be with'. The possessive form *-tʊte* was described as an auxiliary in Gibson (2012) and presumably has its origins in a lexical verb. The construction formed with *-tʊte* can only be used in the perfective and involves an irregular form of imbrication meaning that it appears as *-tʊte* and the usual perfective suffix form *-ire* is not found.

(see Gibson & Wilhelmsen (2015) for a more detailed account of negation in Rangi).

(99) Ka-sɪ-t-óó-vyaal-a   tʊ-sɪ-ker-e   tama   tʊkʊ
     COND-NEG-1pl-PROG-bear-FV SM1PL-NEG-cut-SBJV 9.desire NEG
     'if we do not bear [children], we should not lose hope'
                                                    (Rangi, Stegen 2011: 129)

In both the negative possessive constructions and the negative subjunctive, the marker *tʊkʊ* also appears after the verb, either in the post-verbal or clause-final position. The analysis of these constructions can also be seen to follow from the general account provided for negation in Section 5.4.1 above. The subject marker is projected onto a locally unfixed node. Parsing the negative marker then results in the introduction of the negative polarity value at the root node. In the case of the *sina* construction, parsing *-na* after the negative marker gives rise to the negative possessive reading, whilst *-tɪtɪte* can be considered to be more verb-like in nature and alone be responsible for the provision of the possessive reading (through the annotation of the predicate node with the value Fo(have') for example).

Interestingly, a negative possessive construction can also be formed using the negative marker *sí*. In this case, *tʊkʊ* does not appear in the clause (100).

(100) twa-sina   mpeesa   baa chá-kʊrya
      SM1pl-NEG.have 9.money nor 7-food
      'we do not have money or food'

However, it is proposed here that the same analysis can be maintained due to the presence of the negative word *baa* 'nor' in the clause, which can be proposed to be responsible for the introduction of the negative polarity into the tree, thereby satisfying the negative requirement introduced by *sí*.

5.4.3. *The Rangi negative copula*

The final negative context under examination here is the Rangi negative copula construction. Non-verbal predication in Rangi is typically achieved through the use of either the inflecting copula form *-rɪ* or the non-inflecting copula form *nɪ*.[28] However, negative non-verbal predication can be achieved through the use of the negative forms *sí* and *tʊkʊ* which were also seen in negation in main clause contexts. In non-verbal predication however, it appears that *sí* is the only predicative base in a construction, as in the examples below.

---

[28] The inflecting copula form *-rɪ* is not considered in any more detail here since it is assumed that *-rɪ* functions in a similar manner to a verb stem and introduces the associated structure and interpretation (i.e. *be*).

(101) ʊ-hʊ   sí   mo-osí   Leo tʊkʊ
      1-DEM   NEG   1-old.man   Leo NEG
      'this is not Mr Leo' (Gibson 2012: 95)

(102) weéwe   sí   mʊ-lɩɩhi   tʊkʊ. . .
      2sg.PP   NEG   1-tall   NEG
      'you are not tall. . .' (Gibson 2012: 95)

(103) ɩ-ki   kɩ-kombe sí   ch-aanɩ tʊkʊ, ní   ch-ááchwe
      DEM-7   7-cup   NEG   7-my   NEG   COP   7-his/her
      'this cup is not mine, it is his/hers' (Gibson 2012: 95)

The contribution of negative polarity by the *sí . . . tʊkʊ* structure can be assumed to be the same as that proposed for the preceding construction types. However, the account developed above is not sufficient to be able to capture the use of *sí* as a copula where it provides a fully-specified formula value for the predicate node. In these examples, *sí* appears to function as the entire predicative base for the construction. As such, a slightly different account is needed to be able to model the Rangi negative copula constructions.

Cann et al. (2005b) and Cann (2006, 2007) develop an account of copula constructions in English in which the copula is analysed as projecting an underspecified predicate metavariable **BE**. The node decorated with **BE** is considered to be a predicate node that takes some term as its argument. i.e. it is a $Ty(e \rightarrow (e_s \rightarrow t))$ node. A similar approach is adopted in Seraku (2013b: 166) in which the Japanese copula *da*, at least in cleft constructions, is considered to induce a propositional metavariable which licenses the re-application of actions provided by context. Since Japanese is a verb-final language and the copula can be the last element in the clause, this re-application of the actions provided by the contexts could constitute the actions of a verb, for example, which would serve to further build the propositional structure.

Following this approach, it is proposed here that in negative copula constructions, the Rangi negative form (regardless of whether it is a negative marker or a negative copula) *sí* introduces the metavariable **BE**. Although this metavariable serves as a placeholder, it differs slightly from the other placeholders which are accompanied by the requirement for update to a full formula value (represented by $?\exists x.Fo(x)$) since it allows further update before the parse is complete but this is not obligatory. The **BE** metavariable can therefore be enriched by information from a variety of elements, including adjectives, nominals or even a predicate formula value provided by a verb. However, if no further enrichment is provided, **BE** can persist since its (minimal) semantics are sufficient for a predicative base.

In addition to the introduction of the metavariable **BE**, it is proposed here that *sí* is also responsible for introducing the negative polarity annotation on the root node (consistent with its negative semantics) and for projecting a situation argument node and its corresponding $Ty(e{\rightarrow}(e_s{\rightarrow}t))$ node. The next element to come into parse is projected onto an unfixed node projected from this predicate node. In the case of a adjectival form, such as *mulɪhi* 'tall' in example (102), this information can subsequently provide update for the **BE** predicate node, thereby serving to provide a further enriched annotation for this node. The emergent tree following the parse of *sí* is shown in (104) below.

(104) Parsing: *Weéwe sí muliihi...* 'You are not tall...'

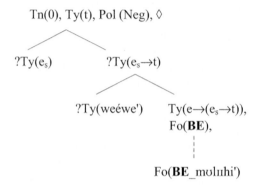

Additional details of the account of negation in Rangi auxiliary constructions are presented in Chapter 6 where it will be seen that the lexical entry for *sí* will need to be further developed in order to account for compound constructions in which negation is associated with the auxiliary-verb order. It is also proposed that the default temporal interpretation of such clauses is present tense, enabling the introduction of the present tense information onto the situation argument node.

This analysis of **BE** and the role it plays in the building of propositional structure, can also be extended in a straightforward manner to account for observations relating to ellipsis in Rangi where it is possible for the second (in this case, negative) clause to appear without an additional copula form (105).

(105) Ní   mbʊrí   vii   noo   ji-chung-irwe   na   ndihi,   ngoombe
       COP 10.goats only COP   SM10-tie-APPL.PASS.PFV   PREP   9.rope   10.cows
       tʊkʊ.
       NEG
       'It is the goats that have been tied with a rope, not the cows'

The proposal is therefore that the predicate node in the LINKed tree (i.e. the one corresponding to the clause without an overt copula form) would receive update from the copula in the main clause (see Kempson et al. 2011a and Purver et al.

2006 for more on ellipsis). Such an analysis assumes that the first clause and the second are connected through a LINK relation, ensuring the flow of information between the two.

5.5. CAPTURING THE HISTORICAL DEVELOPMENT OF BANTU NEGATION MARKERS

There are a number of questions which arise in relation to the modelling of the development of negation strategies in Bantu from a diachronic perspective. Whilst this section does not seek to provide a full account of the historical stages of development that gave rise to the negation systems found in Swahili and Rangi, or indeed Bantu more broadly, it is worth noting some of the ways in which the analyses presented above can be seen to be linked to the historical rise of these structures.

The first issue relates to the apparent syncretism in the forms of the negative marker and the negative copula – *si* in both cases – in Rangi. To introduce a somewhat artificial distinction we can distinguish between the 'negative marker' *si* which serves to encode negation in main clauses declarative negative constructions and the 'negative copula' (also of the form *si*) which can function as a negative predicative base in non-verbal predication. This poses a question both for the synchronic and diachronic analysis of these constructions: how to account for the restrictions in terms of the distributional properties of these forms (and more strictly, the elements with which they can and cannot occur) as well as the distinct contributions to the tree building process that they are proposed to make.

From a synchronic perspective, modelling instances of homophony does not pose a problem for the Dynamic Syntax framework. Rather, a single lexical entry can be proposed for *si*. This lexical item will be associated with a number of different possible triggering contexts which will subsequently give rise to the unfolding of a range of different structures. For example, in both instances, *si* introduces the negative polarity into the clause, so this will be common across the two different uses. However, when *si* is first encountered it is not possible to know whether it will ultimately be followed by a verb (and can thereby be seen as more of a negative marker which does not need to give rise to the unfolding of propositional structure) or whether it will function alone as the sole predicate base (in which case it functions more like a negative copula). For the DS approach, the status of the form as a copula versus marker makes little difference since what is central to the analysis is the linear order in which the elements are encountered and their respective contribution to the tree building process. As such, the lexical entry for *si* is necessarily complex in order to account for the different possible contexts in which it can be parsed. This lexical entry can also contain a disjunction which will allow a sub-set of lexical actions with different triggers.

From a diachronic perspective, Kamba Muzenga (1981: 100–1) explicitly links the pre-initial negative marker to the negative copula in a number of Bantu languages and includes Rangi amongst those languages in which the historical pre-initial *nka/ha* negative marker has been replaced by the negative copula *sí*. Reference has been made to the presence of complex lexical entries (i.e. those involving multiple triggering contexts and associated lexical entries) in DS accounts of the historical processes of language change. Recall that under the DS approach, multiple strategies may be available for parsing an element (or indeed, the whole string) although there must be at least one means of representing the content which gives rise to the propositional output associated with the well-formed natural language string. It is exactly this feature of the DS approach which is used to capture processes associated with language change. Since multiple parsing strategies can be associated with a single string, over time a given pathway can become routinised (in the sense of Pickering & Garrod 2005, as observed by Bouzouita 2008b) with a particular pathway ultimately regularly diverging from a possible initial point of origin.

A related point which can be seen in the current chapter is connected to the number of instances in which negation is marked in the clause. As was seen in the data from both Swahili and Rangi, it is possible for negation to be marked once or twice (and in other Bantu languages even three times as in Salampasu) within the clause. This observation has been linked to manifestations of Jespersen's cycle across Bantu (Devos et al. 2010; Devos & van der Auwera 2013; Gibson & Wilhelmsen 2015). Such cyclical processes of change can naturally be accounted for under the Dynamic Syntax approach. What may have started out life as an emphatic marker of negation can over time grammaticalise to become an obligatory proponent of negation. In DS terms, this could be captured by reference to the introduction of a requirement for negative polarity (such as ?Pol(Neg)) and then the second marker being responsible for introducing this negative polarity, as was proposed to be the case for Rangi. As a result of this process of change, the associated pragmatics of 'emphasis' may ultimately be eroded. This would result in the doubling marking becoming the standard way of encoding negation. It is therefore a natural step for another negative word (which may have its origins in a range of different sources, including negative answer words, degree words, locatives, possessives, etc.) to be used to emphasise the negative polarity. In DS terms, this marker of negation is either still a lexical word which makes the appropriate lexically-specified contribution to the clause, or it satisfies a requirement introduced by an earlier element in the clause, and over time the construction as a whole routinises to become the standard negative pattern.

In this way, the powerful concepts of context-dependency, as well as the underspecification which is conferred by the complex lexical entries of all morphemes in a string, can be seen to capture the process of language change associated with the rise of negative constructions. Individual elements are considered to make their own lexically-specified contribution to the parsing/

production process. However, these elements are not considered to make a singular, fixed contribution to this process, but rather their contribution to the clause is dependent on the contents that are present in the tree at the point when it is parsed. The lexical entry can therefore be seen to reflect the variety of possible triggering contexts, as well as a possibly broad range of actions that can be induced as a result of the parse.

5.6. SUMMARY

This chapter has provided an exploration of the issues involved in parsing negative constructions in the Bantu languages, with a focus on Swahili and Rangi. Whilst in many instances the analyses presented here can be extended to other Bantu languages, the challenges represented by the micro-variation attested in the language family will no doubt extend to include the formal account of negation. However, it seems that in general, segmental morphological markers of negation can be modelled as introducing a negative interpretation into the clause (in the current study this was associated only with the naïve representation of negative polarity as Pol(Neg) at the root node). Such markers may also be considered to be responsible for the construction of a situation argument node (as was proposed to be the case for Swahili) reflecting the interaction between negation and tense-aspect marking, as well as enabling the necessary conditions for parsing the verb stem. However, the presence of more than one marker of negation may mean that an analysis in which only one such item is responsible for encoding the negative polarity and the other element simply introduces a requirement for this negative meaning (as was proposed for Rangi), is also justified. In this way, independent negative particles may not interact with the clause beyond the introduction of the negative polarity and may therefore necessitate only an analysis under which they introduce this meaning but do not build any structure nor provide an update to structural relations.

The current chapter does not examine languages which have negative auxiliaries, but these can presumably be modelled in a similar way to negative markers (much in the same way as tense-aspect auxiliaries were modelled in a similar way to tense-aspect markers). If auxiliaries are assumed to be more verb-like in nature, and are often more transparently related to the lexical verbs from which they are derived, there may be further justification for proposing that they are responsible for introducing more substantial predicate-argument structure, whilst also making a negative polarity contribution to the tree.

Overall, the analysis presented here uses a *pro tem* representation of negation in which negation is shown merely through a diacritic on the root node. However, there have been suggestions that a formal account of negation could include the concept of 'no witness' and that negation could be encoded on the situation argument node, reflecting the interaction between tense-aspect and negation. Alternatively, structure above the root node could be used to represent the illocutionary force of an utterance (denial in the case of negation) as noted by Lucas (2014). If we allow the possibility that negation may be expressed at more than one location in the tree, then it becomes possible to distinguish lexical items in terms of where they make their contribution to the negative polarity of the sentence. In either case, the contribution of a negative element – a negative particle, negative word or negative morphology – is to be represented high up in the tree at the root node, or at the situation argument node. This reflects the observation that in DS terms, individual lexical items are not negative per se, although they may well be associated with negative readings. Rather, it is propositions that are negative.

6

MODELLING AUXILIARY PLACEMENT
IN RANGI

Rangi exhibits a typologically and comparatively unusual word order in which the auxiliary appears after the main verb in restricted syntactic contexts. This word order is marked in the context of East African Bantu where auxiliary-verb order predominates. It is also unusual from a broader comparative typological perspective where SVO languages are expected to exhibit pre-verbal auxiliary placement. Moreover, whilst declarative main clauses exhibit verb-auxiliary order, this order is inverted in a specific set of contexts. This results in an alternation between pre-verbal and post-verbal auxiliary placement.

This chapter provides a formal analysis of this unusual word order and the associated alternation found in Rangi. Under the DS approach, this word order alternation can be considered to be the result of an independent constraint operative in the system which prohibits the co-existence of more than one unfixed node at any point in the parsing process, thereby serving to curtail underspecification. The analysis presented in this chapter shows the context-dependent nature of structure building and the power of the manipulation of underspecified content. The account also highlights the centrality of procedural constraints and the ways in which these are manifested cross-linguistically. This is a point which is expanded on in Chapter 7.

6.1. Bantu auxiliary constructions

Bantu languages regularly use sequences of verbs to express a wide array of tense-aspect-mood combinations. Simple forms comprise of a single verb typically inflected for tense and/or aspect through a combination of markers and, where applicable, an associated tone pattern. Auxiliary constructions comprise of two or more verb forms (or elements of verbal origin) in which at least one makes a grammatical rather than a lexical contribution to the clause. In some Bantu languages, each of the verbs in an auxiliary verb construction carries agreement with the subject of the clause as can be seen in the examples below from Swahili (106), Hehe (107) and siSwati (108).

(106) Wa-li-kuwa wa-me-fika
     SM2-PAST-be SM2-PERF-arrive-FV
     'they had arrived' (Swahili)

(107) Saa tu-va tu-gus-ile
come.FUT SM1pl-be SM1pl-buy-RETR
'we will have bought' (Hehe, Nurse 2003: 91)

(108) Leli-hhashi la-phose   ku-ngi-wis-a
DEM5-5.horse SM5.PST-almost INF-OM1sg-throw-FV
'this horse nearly threw me' (siSwati, Ziervogel & Mabuza 1976: 151)

A range of grammaticalisation processes have resulted in variation in Bantu auxiliary constructions in a number of regards. Subject-marking properties, the distribution of tense-aspect-mood information across the elements and the number of auxiliaries present in a given language all show a high level of variation across the language family. Amidst this variation, auxiliary-verb order dominates across the language family. However, an exception to this generalisation can be found in a small group of Bantu languages spoken in East Africa. In these languages verb-auxiliary order is associated with certain tense-aspect combinations and an attempt at the more Bantu-typical auxiliary-verb order in these contexts renders the utterance ungrammatical. Rangi is one such language.

In compound verbal constructions in most Bantu languages, the first element is an auxiliary, whilst the second element is the main lexical verb. This is also the case in Rangi in a number of tenses. Thus, the recent past perfective is formed using the auxiliary -rɪ and is followed by an inflected main verb, as can be seen in example (109) below. Similarly, the distant past perfective is formed using the auxiliary -íja in conjunction with a lexical main verb and exhibits the Bantu-typical auxiliary-verb order (110).

(109) U-ra mʊ-gonjwa áá-rɪ   a-a-kwíy-ire.
1-DEM 1-ill.person SM1-AUX.PAST1 SM1-PAST1-die-PTV
'that ill person has died'   (Rangi, Gibson 2012: 43)

(110) A-íja   mʊ-dúúdi a-íja
SM1-AUX.PAST2 1-small SM1-AUX.PAST2
i-i-fyeen-ire   na íyo w-aavo.
SM1-REFL-ressemble-PERF CONN 1a.mother SM1a-their
'when s/he was small s/he looked like their mother'
             (Rangi, Gibson 2012: 96)

However, in addition to this more Bantu-typical auxiliary-verb order, Rangi also exhibits post-verbal auxiliary placement as can be seen in (111) and (112) below where at attempt at pre-verbal placement of the auxiliary results in ungrammaticality (113).

(111) Kw-i-súm-ʊl-a   n-íise   i-hi   mbʊ́ri   haaha.
       INF-OM9-take-SEP-FV SM1sg-AUX.FUT 9-DEM 9.goat now
       'I will take this goat now' (Rangi, Gibson 2012: 71)

(112) Mama   jót-a   a-rɪ   maaji   mpolɪ.
       1.mother   collect-FV   SM1-AUX   6.water later
       'mother will collect water later' (Rangi, Gibson 2012: 110)

(113) *N-íise   térek-a   chá-kʊ́rya.
       SM1sg-AUX.FUT   cook-FV   7-food
       'I will cook food' (Rangi, Gibson 2012: 17)

6.2. Modelling Rangi auxiliary constructions

The first challenge is how to model auxiliary constructions in Bantu in general. The majority of compound constructions in the language family exhibit auxiliary-verb order, in line with the cross-linguistic expectation for SVO languages. The proposal developed here is that the auxiliary projects fixed predicate-argument structure and that the verb projects fixed predicate-argument structure which subsequently collapses onto the structure introduced by the auxiliary. The subject markers on both forms are identical in terms of noun class (or person and number) information, and collapse onto the same node, indicating the co-referential nature of these elements.

The Rangi distant past perfective is formed using an auxiliary construction. The auxiliary *-ija* appears in combination with a verb form inflected for perfective aspect by the suffix *-ire*. Whilst the main verb carries the lexical and aspectual information, the auxiliary locates the event in the distant past. Both the auxiliary and the main verb are inflected for subject information, as can be seen in example (114) below.

(114) Mama   a-íja   a-dóm-ire
       1a.mother SM1-AUX.PAST2   SM1.PAST2-go-PTV
       'mother has gone'

Parsing the subject expression results in the establishment of a parallel tree annotated with the formula value – in this case Fo(mama') (see Chapter 3). This parallel tree is connected to the main tree via a LINK relation and will ultimately provide the background for the interpretation of the subject marker on the verb form. In fact, in the case of these auxiliary constructions there will be two subject markers – one which is associated with the auxiliary form and one which is associated with the main verb form. Parsing the subject marker on the auxiliary results in the projection of a locally unfixed node annotated with a metavariable placeholder. In the case of the current example, parsing *a-* encodes the restriction that this metavariable receives interpretation from a class 1 noun. The expression *mama* 'mother' on the LINK structure provides the necessary contextual information for the interpretation of the metavariable on the locally unfixed node, enabling immediate update to the full formula value Fo(mama'). The resulting tree is shown in (115) below.

(115) Parsing: *Mama a-...* 'Mother...'

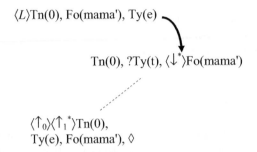

$\langle L \rangle$Tn(0), Fo(mama'), Ty(e)

Tn(0), ?Ty(t), $\langle \downarrow^* \rangle$Fo(mama')

$\langle \uparrow_0 \rangle \langle \uparrow_1{}^* \rangle$Tn(0),
Ty(e), Fo(mama'), $\Diamond$

Recall that Bantu tense-aspect markers are modelled as contributing fixed structure to the tree and as introducing tense and/or aspect information to the semantic representation established during the parse (Kempson & Marten 2002, Gibson 2012). Following on from this claim, here the auxiliary *-ija* is analysed as contributing distant past tense information to the clause and projecting a fixed subject node and a fixed predicate node (much in the same way as tense-aspect markers). The introduction of fixed structure by the auxiliary follows the analysis of the English copula *be* provided by Cann (2011) in which *be* is assumed to project fixed predicate-argument structure. This account also reflects the historical origin of Bantu auxiliary forms in main verbs which are modelled in similar terms (see, for example, Marten et al. 2008 and Gibson 2012 for DS analyses of Bantu auxiliaries from this perspective). The lexical entry for *-ija* is provided in (116) below.[29]

(116) Lexical entry for the distant past auxiliary *-ija*

> *-ija* IF   ?Ty(t), $\langle \downarrow_1{}^* \rangle \langle \downarrow_0 \rangle$Ty(e)
>   THEN   make($\langle \downarrow_0 \rangle$); go($\langle \downarrow_0 \rangle$); put(Ty(e), Fo(S$_\text{DISTANT PAST}$));
>   go($\langle \uparrow_0 \rangle$); make($\langle \downarrow_1 \rangle$); go($\langle \downarrow_1 \rangle$); put(?Ty(e$_s$→t));
>   make($\langle \downarrow_1 \rangle$); go($\langle \downarrow_1 \rangle$);
>   put((Ty(e→(e$_s$→t)), Fo(**W**), ?∃x.Fo(x)); go($\langle \uparrow_1 \rangle$);
>   make($\langle \downarrow_0 \rangle$); go($\langle \downarrow_0 \rangle$); put(?Ty(e))
>   ELSE   abort

---

[29] Note here that it is assumed that as part of this historical development of the auxiliary *-ija*, the final *-a* has been re-analysed from a distinct inflectional suffix (as the final vowel on what is presumed historically to have been a main verb) to form part of the auxiliary form.

As can be seen on examination of the lexical entry in (116) above, the lexical trigger for parsing the auxiliary -*ija* is the requirement for a propositional value – ?Ty(t) – and the presence of a locally unfixed argument node ($\langle\downarrow_1^*\rangle\langle\downarrow_0\rangle$Ty(e)). This reflects the observation that at the point at which the auxiliary is parsed, no fixed structure is present in the tree and that the auxiliary is obligatorily prefixed by a subject marker. When these conditions are met, parsing the auxiliary -*ija* results in the projection of a fixed subject node and a fixed predicate node annotated with the metavariable placeholder, for example, Fo(**W**). The presence of the metavariable on the predicate node indicates that parsing the auxiliary does not provide a full predicate formula value but that one must be introduced before the parse is complete. The metavariable can later be substituted by the information provided by the main verb, much in the same way as substitution of a metavariable introduced by a pronoun or a noun class marker occurs. The auxiliary also introduces a situation argument node which can be immediately annotated with the past tense information (since -*ija* can be analysed as a dedicated distant past tense marker which is not used in the formation of any other tense forms).

Following the introduction of the fixed subject node, the locally unfixed node collapses with the subject node, providing a fixed tree node address for the subject. The metavariable on the predicate node remains until the main verb is parsed. The resulting tree following the parsing of the auxiliary and the induction of the fixed predicate-argument structure is shown in (117) below.

(117)　Parsing: *Mama a-ija*...

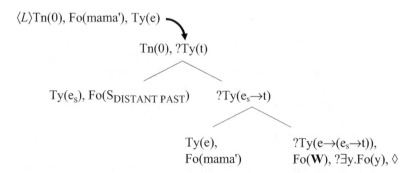

The next element to be parsed in a distant past perfective auxiliary construction is the subject marker on the main verb. The lexical entry detailed in Chapter 3 indicates that Rangi subject markers can only be parsed if there is no fixed structure present in the tree at the point when they are encountered (recall that the lexical trigger for parsing the subject marker is the requirement for a locally unfixed node i.e. ?Ty(e),$\langle\uparrow_0\rangle\langle\uparrow_1^*\rangle$?Ty(t). However, in compound constructions when the main verb comes to be parsed, the auxiliary has already introduced fixed structure into the tree. Moreover, the application of the rule of LOCAL *ADJUNCTION, which would induce the locally unfixed node onto which the subject marker is projected has also previously been restricted to clause-initial contexts. The lexical entry provided for Rangi subject markers therefore has to account for the possibility of the subject marker being parsed in the presence of fixed structure. However, the possible occurrence of this must be restricted to ensure that it only takes place when the fixed structure has been introduced by an auxiliary. This is to limit potential over-generation and to prohibit the licensing of ungrammatical constructions, such as ones in which a subject marker is projected onto a locally unfixed node after the introduction of fixed structure, but not in an auxiliary construction.

In order to encode this restriction in formal terms, the subject marker is analysed as projecting a locally unfixed node when it is parsed in the presence of a $Ty(e)$ node annotated with a predicate metavariable (which in these constructions would have already been introduced by the auxiliary). The lexical entry for the Rangi class 1 subject marker a- is shown in (118) below.

(118)   Lexical entry for Rangi subject marker a-

a-	IF	$?Ty(t)$
THEN	IF	$[\downarrow]\bot$
	THEN	make($\langle\downarrow_1*\rangle\langle\downarrow_0\rangle$); go($\langle\downarrow_1*\rangle\langle\downarrow_0\rangle$);
		put($Ty(e)$, $Fo(U_{CLASS1})$, $?\exists x.Fo(x)$)
ELSE	IF	$\langle\downarrow_1\rangle(Ty(e\rightarrow t)$, $Fo(V)$, $?\exists x.Fo(x)$)
	THEN	go($\langle\downarrow_0\rangle$); put($Ty(e)$), $Fo(U_{CLASS1})$, $?\exists y.Fo(y)$)
	ELSE	abort

The subject marker has a $?Ty(t)$ node as its general lexical trigger. Further restriction on the parsing of the subject marker is captured by the two IF clauses. The first IF clause states that in the absence of any fixed structure, parsing the subject marker results in the projection of a locally unfixed node annotated with the restricted metavariable. The second IF clause provides that in the presence of such a predicate metavariable, parsing the subject marker will result only in the annotation of the subject node with a restricted metavariable.

In order for the utterance to be well-formed, the subject marker on the auxiliary and on the main verb must be of the same noun class (or encode the same person and number distinctions). The re-decoration of the subject node with the information provided by the second subject marker ensures the co-referentiality of these subject markers since they annotate the same node of the same semantic tree. Not only is the re-construction of structure therefore possible within Dynamic Syntax, in this context it is essential to ensure that the subject markers refer to the same entity. If the subject markers do not agree in terms of noun class, the parse will fail at this point.

The lexical entry for the intransitive use of the predicate *-dom-* 'go' is shown in (119) below.

(119) Lexical entry for the Rangi verb *-dom-* 'go'

-dom-   IF $?Ty(e{\rightarrow}t))$
         THEN $go(\langle\uparrow_0\rangle)$; $make(\langle\downarrow_0\rangle)$; $go(\langle\downarrow_0\rangle)$;
                 $put(Ty(e), Fo(\mathbf{U}), ?\exists x.Fo(x))$;
                 $go(\langle\uparrow_0\rangle)$; $go(\langle\downarrow_1\rangle)$; $put(Ty(e{\rightarrow}t), Fo(dom'))$;
         ELSE   abort

Parsing the verb stem builds fixed predicate-argument structure, resulting in the introduction of the lexical semantic content into the tree. The fixed subject and fixed predicate nodes introduced by the verb stem collapse with the fixed structure which has been introduced by the auxiliary. Parsing the verb also enables the update of the metavariable placeholder on the predicate node to a full formula value. In the case of a transitive predicate, the verb constructs a predicate node and its corresponding object argument node. The resulting tree structure can be seen in (120) below.

(120) Parsing: *a-íja a-dóm-...*

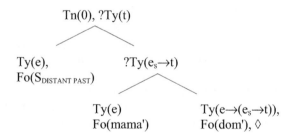

$Tn(0), ?Ty(t)$

$Ty(e),$
$Fo(S_{\text{DISTANT PAST}})$

$?Ty(e_s{\rightarrow}t)$

$Ty(e)$
$Fo(mama')$

$Ty(e{\rightarrow}(e_s{\rightarrow}t)),$
$Fo(dom'), \Diamond$

The verb stem ends with an obligatory suffix – either the default so-called final vowel *-a* or a dedicated temporal-aspectual suffix. In this example, parsing the perfective suffix *-ire* on the main verb results in the introduction of perfective aspect to the clause. This information annotates the situation argument node. Parsing *-ire* also indicates the end of the verbal form and means that no further predicate nodes can be constructed. With all the requirements fulfilled, the information is compiled up the tree. The final stage in the derivation is shown in the semantic tree in (121) below.

(121) Parsing: (*Mama*)   *a-íja*   *a-dóm-ire*
                1a.mother SM1-AUX.PAST2 SM1.PAST2-go-PTV
                'Mother has gone'

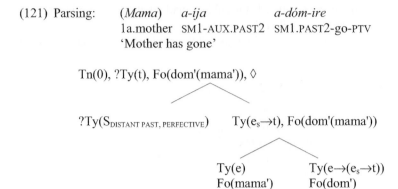

A similar account can be extended to other uses of the distant past auxiliary *-ija* which is also used to form the distant past habitual which employs the habitual suffix *-áa*, as can be seen in (122) below.

(122) Tw-íja   twá-kikal-áa   Kondoa
      SM1pl-AUX.PAST2 SM1pl.PAST2-stay-HAB Kondoa
      'we used to live in Kondoa' (Dunham 2005: 157)

Modelling example (122) would proceed in the same manner as has been shown for the distant past perfective form above, but when the suffix *-áa* is parsed, a habitual annotation is introduced on the situation argument node.

The analysis presented above for the Rangi auxiliary *-íja*, which it is argued can in fact be extended to other Bantu auxiliaries which participate in the standard auxiliary-verb construction (see also Gibson & Marten 2016), is based on the assumption that constructions involving the past tense auxiliary *-íja* are monoclausal. This means that a single semantic structure is built, even in the case of compound verbal constructions such as those associated with auxiliary forms. Under this approach, a single semantic representation is employed for both the structure induced by parsing the auxiliary and that induced by parsing the main verb. The resulting tree structure has just one predicate-argument structure (although of any possible valency), which may be annotated with complex temporal and aspectual information as determined by the information that is distributed across the forms. Such an analysis is motivated by two considerations. The first relates to the interaction between auxiliary constructions and the broader tense-aspect system in the languages, while the second is based on the historical connection between auxiliaries and main verbs.

First, it is proposed here that the use of compound-based auxiliary constructions enables languages to express a broader range of complex tense-aspect information as a single event than would be possible solely through the use of a simple verb forms. In Swahili for example, since there is only a pre-stem position available for the encoding of temporal and aspectual information, the use of auxiliary forms enables the encoding of a wider range of distinctions which would not otherwise be possible in a single verb form.

Second, the proposal of a monoclausal analysis for auxiliary constructions is also based on the historical origin of auxiliary forms and the connection between auxiliaries, main verbs and tense-aspect markers. Auxiliaries have been noted to have their origins in lexical verbs across Bantu languages (Botne 1989), with many Bantu tense-aspect markers in turn having developed from grammaticalised auxiliary forms, as has been noted for Swahili (see Meinhof 1899; Sacleux 1909; 172; Ashton 1944: 205; Miehe 1979: 204ff; Botne 1989; Heine & Reh 1984:130; Heine et al. 1991). In Rangi, the iterative marker *-endo-* appears to have its historical origins in the main verb *kweenda* 'go' (Dunham 2005:154), whilst it has been proposed that the auxiliary form *-ija* is derived from the verb *-vja* 'come' (Stegen 2001).

In the formal modelling of *-ija* provided above, the auxiliary is analysed as introducing fixed predicate-argument structure and temporal information. However, in contrast to a main verb, it does not make any contribution in terms of the lexico-semantics of the predicate. In this regard, since the auxiliary is bleached of other semantic content, it behaves more like a tense-aspect marker than a verb. In terms of structural contribution however, Rangi auxiliaries pattern with both verbs and tense-aspect markers, which are also responsible for building fixed-predicate argument structure. A comparison of the formal characteristics of Rangi inflected verbs, auxiliary forms and tense-aspect markers is provided in Table 2.

Table 2 shows the lexical triggers and lexical actions associated with Rangi tense-aspect markers, auxiliaries and main verb stems. Pre-stem tense-aspect markers are parsed in the presence of a locally unfixed node and no fixed

Table 2. Contribution made by TA makers, verb stems and auxiliaries to the structure building process

	Lexical trigger	Lexical actions
Pre-stem TA marker	A locally unfixed node and no fixed structure	(i) Build fixed minimal predicate-argument frame (ii) build fixed situation argument node (iii) Provide tense-aspect annotation for situation argument node
Auxiliary	A locally unfixed node with subject annotation	(i) Build fixed subject node (ii) Build fixed predicate node annotated with a metavariable (iii) Introduce tense-aspect information (where relevant)
Verb stem	Predicate-requiring node	(i) Build fixed predicate-argument structure (ii) Provide full formula annotation for predicate node

structure. When these triggering conditions are met, parsing the tense-aspect marker results in the construction of fixed minimal predicate-argument structure and the introduction of a situation argument annotated with the corresponding tense-aspect information. The same lexical trigger is proposed for auxiliaries although parsing an auxiliary form requires subject information to be present in the tree. Parsing the auxiliary results in the projection of fixed minimal predicate-argument structure. Unlike tense-aspect markers however, auxiliaries introduce a metavariable on the predicate node, which requires update to a full formula value which can only be achieved when the main verb is parsed.

Verb stems have a predicate requiring node as their lexical trigger. The lexical actions induced by verbs result in the construction of fixed predicate-argument structure. Parsing verb stems provides the semantic-conceptual contribution to the clause and enables update to a full formula value for a metavariable on the predicate node. Structurally, verbs and auxiliaries pattern together. However, in terms of making a temporal contribution, auxiliaries also pattern with tense-aspect markers. The similarities between the structure induced by tense-aspect markers, lexical verbs and auxiliaries reflects the historical relation between these elements.

Finally, the analysis of compound verbal constructions presented here provides support for a pronoun-like characterisation of the subject marker. In the analysis presented by Bresnan & Mchombo (1987), Bantu subject markers are considered to be ambiguous between anaphoric and grammatical agreement. The DS analysis of Bantu subject markers is also affected by this criticism since it assumes that subject markers are interpreted more like pronouns. By employing the notions of underspecification and update as they allow for the re-building of semantic structure in highly constrained conditions, Bantu subject markers can be seen as pronouns which can be interpreted from context. This is only possible however if the interpretation of the second subject marker is highly restricted, with both the subject marker on the auxiliary and the subject marker on the main verb analysed as agreeing with the overt subject of the entire verbal complex (this is the proposal that was also made by Gibson & Marten 2016).[30]

6.2.1. Modelling the Rangi verb-auxiliary order

This section builds on the analysis of the auxiliary constructions presented above for past tense auxiliary -ija and provides an account of the constructions which exhibit the verb-auxiliary order and the associated alternation.

Recall that the typologically and comparatively usual verb-auxiliary order is found in Rangi only in the immediate and general future tense forms. The immediate future is formed through use of an infinitive and the auxiliary -iise (123), whilst the general future is formed using the auxiliary -rɪ (124). In both

---

[30] This pronoun-like characterisation of the Bantu subject marker is not without its problems since it still requires a decision to be made in terms of a pronominal or an agreement analysis of the subject marker. However, such a marker can naturally be interpreted from context in line with the DS general approach to interpretation without the need to posit an additional empty category.

constructions, the auxiliary consistently follows the main verb in declarative main clauses.[31]

(123) Nıínı   lʊ́ʊ́s-a   n-íise   a-ha   víí
      1sg.PP speak-FV SM1sg-AUX.FUT DEM-16 just
      'I will talk soon'

(124) Jót-a   á-rɪ   maaji   mpolı
      gather-FV SM1-AUX   6.water   later
      's/he will get water later'

Following on from the analysis of the auxiliary -ija, the auxiliary -iise is analysed as projecting fixed minimal predicate-argument structure, as well as contributing immediate future tense to a clause. However, in order to capture the ordering of the auxiliary and the verb, it is proposed that the infinitive appearing in the initial position is projected onto an unfixed predicate node. Whilst this unfixed predicate node is annotated with a full formula value as provided by the infinitive, it does not receive a fixed tree node address until the auxiliary is parsed (thereby introducing fixed structure into the tree for the first time).

When the infinitival verb form is parsed as the first element, it provides the annotation for an unfixed $Ty(e{\to}t)$ predicate node introduced by the rule of PREDICATE ADJUNCTION. The rule of PREDICATE ADJUNCTION was defined in Gibson (2012) to account for the projection of an unfixed predicate node for which no formal provision had previously been made within the Dynamic Syntax framework. The rule of PREDICATE ADJUNCTION induces an unfixed $?Ty(e{\to}t)$ node from a query type t node. The introduction of this rule was argued to be a natural extension of the DS framework, which already provided for unfixed argument nodes and which recognised different types (Kempson et al. 2001; Cann et al. 2005b), meaning that the new rule was consistent with the overall architecture of the DS system. More specifically however, in Gibson (2012) it was argued that the verb-auxiliary constructions found in Rangi necessitated the extension of the DS framework to include the notion of an unfixed predicate node. The rule was defined in formal terms as in (125) below.

(125) The rule of PREDICATE ADJUNCTION (as defined in Gibson (2012))

$$\{...\{\{Tn(a),...,?Ty(t), \Diamond\}\}...\}$$

$$\{...\{\{Tn(a),...,?Ty(t)\}, \{\langle\uparrow^*\rangle Tn(a), ?\exists x.Tn(x),...?Ty(e{\to}t), \Diamond\}\}...\}$$

---

[31] As will be seen later in this sub-section, interrogative and negative constructions, as well as relative and subordinate clauses exhibit pre-verbal auxiliary placement in both the immediate future and general future tenses.

Following the application of the rule of PREDICATE ADJUNCTION, the infinitive is projected onto an unfixed $Ty(e{\to}t)$ node, which it annotates with a full formula value. Parsing the infinitive also licenses the construction of fixed predicate-argument structure. In the case of the intransitive predicate, this results in the construction of a $Ty(e{\to}t)$ node and the annotation of this predicate node with the formula value $Fo(l\acute{o}\acute{o}s')$. The lexical entry for the infinitive *lóósa* 'speak' is shown below (based on Chatzikyriakidis & Gibson (2017)).

(126) Lexical entry for a Rangi transitive verb

$l\acute{o}\acute{o}s$- IF $?Ty(e{\to}t)$
    THEN $make(\langle\downarrow_0\rangle)$; $go(\langle\downarrow_0\rangle)$, $put(?Ty(e))$; $go(\langle\uparrow_0\rangle)$;
         $make(\langle\downarrow_1\rangle)$; $go(\langle\downarrow_1\rangle)$; $put(?Ty(e{\to}t))$; $make(\langle\downarrow_0\rangle)$;
         $go(\langle\downarrow_0\rangle)$; $put(?Ty(e))$; $go(\langle\uparrow_0\rangle)$; $make(\langle\downarrow_1\rangle)$; $go(\langle\downarrow_1\rangle)$;
         $put(?Ty(e{\to}(e{\to}t))$ $Fo(l\acute{o}\acute{o}s')$; $go(\langle\uparrow_1\rangle)$; $make(\langle\downarrow_0\rangle)$;
         $go(\langle\downarrow_0\rangle)$; $put(?Ty(e))$
    ELSE   abort

Note here that the verb stem is not analysed as being responsible for the projection of a situation argument since the verb stem itself does not encode any tense-aspect information. In the case of an auxiliary construction, the situation argument node will be introduced by the auxiliary form, whilst in a clause marked with a tense-aspect marker the situation argument will be introduced by this marker. Following the parse of a verb such as *lóósa* 'speak', the resulting structure is that of a one-place predicate as in (127) below.

(127) Parsing: *Lóósa...* 'speak...'

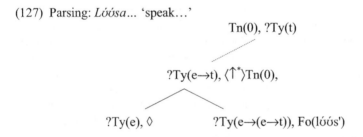

$Tn(0)$, $?Ty(t)$

$?Ty(e{\to}t)$, $\langle\uparrow^*\rangle Tn(0)$,

$?Ty(e)$, $\Diamond$ $?Ty(e{\to}(e{\to}t))$, $Fo(l\acute{o}\acute{o}s')$

The auxiliary form *niise* is the next element to be parsed. The pointer moves to the root node via ANTICIPATION. Parsing the subject marker on the auxiliary form results in the projection of a locally unfixed node annotated with a restricted metavariable. The restricted metavariable limits the possible referents from which the metavariable can receive interpretation, in terms of noun class or person and number distinctions.[32] Since the subject marker *n-* encodes first

---

[32] Omission of the subject is widespread in Rangi. However, in instances in which an overt subject expression is present, it can be projected onto a LINK structure as outlined in Section 2. The subsequent stages of the parse proceed in line with the account provided in the current section and the LINK structure has no bearing on the availability of this strategy.

person singular information, this metavariable can be immediately updated to the content *speaker'* and can be identified with a real-world referent. The partial tree that results at this stage therefore comprises of the node annotated with the predicate *lóósa* 'speak' and a locally unfixed node decorated with information about the potential subject marker expression *speaker'*.

(128) Parsing: *Lóósa n-*... 'Speak...'

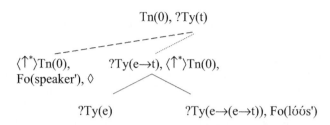

Tn(0), ?Ty(t)

$\langle\uparrow^*\rangle$Tn(0), Fo(speaker'), $\Diamond$

?Ty(e→t), $\langle\uparrow^*\rangle$Tn(0),

?Ty(e)   ?Ty(e→(e→t)), Fo(lóós')

Parsing the subject marker results in the projection of a locally unfixed node annotated with a restricted metavariable determined by the noun class of the subject marker. These two nodes can co-exist due to their different modalities – one is an unfixed predicate node whilst the other is a locally unfixed node. The subject marker can be parsed since there is still no fixed structure present in the tree at this stage. Parsing the auxiliary also introduces a fixed subject node and a fixed predicate node.

(129) Lexical entry for the Rangi auxiliary *-íise*

> *-íise* IF   ?Ty, $\langle\downarrow^*\rangle\langle\downarrow_0\rangle$Ty(e)
>   THEN   make($\langle\downarrow_0\rangle$); go($\langle\downarrow_0\rangle$); put(Ty($e_s$), Fo($S_{IMM\ FUTURE}$));
>   go($\langle\uparrow_0\rangle$); make($\langle\downarrow_1\rangle$); go($\langle\downarrow_1\rangle$); put(Ty($e_s$→t), make($\langle\downarrow_0\rangle$));
>   go($\langle\downarrow_0\rangle$); put(?Ty(e)) go($\langle\uparrow_0\rangle$); make($\langle\downarrow_1\rangle$); go($\langle\downarrow_1\rangle$);
>   put(Fo(**W**), Ty(e→(e_s→t)), ∃y.Fo(y)); go($\langle\uparrow_1\rangle$), go($\langle\downarrow_0\rangle$)
>   ELSE   abort

The fixed structure introduced by the auxiliary enables the establishment of a fixed tree node address for the information introduced by the infinitival verb. Parsing the auxiliary also results in the building of the situation argument node and introduces the immediate future tense annotation. The presence of this structure enables the fixing of the tree node address of the previously unfixed node and identifies the node annotated with Fo(speaker') as the subject of the clause. In the presence of the predicate annotation *lóósa* 'speak' the metavariable introduced by the auxiliary can receive immediate update to a full formula value. At this point in the parse all the tree node addresses are fully-specified and the requirements fulfilled, meaning that the information can be compiled up the tree. The resulting structure is shown in (130).

(130)   Parsing: *lóósa niise* 'I will plant millet.'

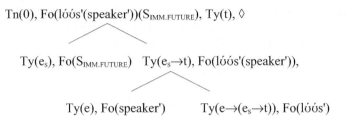

Tn(0), Fo(lóós'(speaker'))(S_{IMM.FUTURE}), Ty(t), ◊

Ty(e$_s$), Fo(S$_{IMM.FUTURE}$)   Ty(e$_s$→t), Fo(lóós'(speaker')),

Ty(e), Fo(speaker')   Ty(e→(e$_s$→t)), Fo(lóós')

It is proposed here that a similar account can be extended to modelling the general future tense. However, there is a crucial difference between the immediate future tense construction and the general future tense which has an impact on the formal modelling. Whilst the use of the auxiliary *-iise* is restricted to the immediate future tense, the auxiliary *-rɪ* which is used to form the general future tense is also used in a number of other tense-aspect combinations. Specifically, *-rɪ* is also used in the present tense where it functions as a standard attributive copula, as well as being used in the past tense where it is used in the past perfective construction. The challenge then in analysing the general future tense comes, not from modelling the word order pattern – which can be accounted for in terms similar to that of the immediate future – but in capturing the specifics of the temporal interpretation with which it is associated. Moreover, in its future tense usage, *-rɪ* is not inflected for temporal or aspectual distinctions, rather it appears that the marked verb-auxiliary order itself is responsible for encoding the future tense interpretation.

As with the analysis of the immediate future tense presented above, it is proposed that in the general future tense, the lexical trigger for the infinitival verb form is an unfixed predicate node introduced via the rule of PREDICATE ADJUNCTION. Parsing the infinitival verb form results in the annotation of this unfixed predicate node with the lexico-semantic information encoded by the verb. In the case of a transitive predicate such as *jóta* 'collect', parsing the infinitive also licenses the construction of an object argument node and a Ty(e→ (e→t)) predicate node. The preliminary lexical entry for the infinitival verb form *jóta* 'collect' is shown in (131) below.

(131)   Lexical entry for the infinite *jóta*

> *jóta*   IF   ?Ty(t), ⟨↓*⟩?Ty(e→t)
>   THEN   go(⟨↓*⟩); make(⟨↓$_1$⟩); go(⟨↓$_1$⟩);
>   put(Ty(e→(e→t)), Fo(jot'));
>   go(⟨↑$_1$⟩); make(⟨↓$_0$⟩); go(⟨↓$_0$⟩); put(?Ty(e));
>   go(⟨↑$_0$⟩);
>   . . .
>   ELSE   abort

As can be seen on examination of the lexical entry above, the infinitive projects a predicate node and an object argument node (since *jota* 'collect' is transitive). However, it does not project a subject node, reflecting the fact that the interpretation of the subject is not provided by the infinitival verb form. The resulting tree can be seen in (132) below, where the underspecified tree node relation represented by the unfixed predicate node dominates the transitive Ty(e→(e→t)) node.

(132) Parsing: *jóta* … 'Collect…'

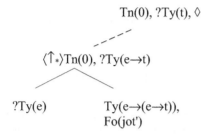

As can be seen in the tree above, whilst the address of the predicate node is unfixed in relation to the top node (represented by the annotation ⟨↑*⟩Tn(0)), this node dominates fixed tree structure. This reflects the fact that whilst the relationship between the predicate node and the root node is not known at this early stage in the derivation, the relation between the subject-requiring node and the predicate nodes is set from the outset since they are both projected by the verb *jóta*. In line with the account presented for the other auxiliaries, parsing the subject marker on the auxiliary projects a locally unfixed node annotated with a restricted metavariable and the auxiliary projects fixed minimal predicate-argument structure. However, the specific temporal interpretation is considered to stem from parsing *-rɪ* in the presence of the unfixed predicate node – a restriction which is captured in its lexical entry shown in (133) below.

(133) Lexical entry for *-rɪ* (in its future tense use)

> *-rɪ* IF   ?Ty(t), ⟨↓*⟩?Ty(e→t)
>   THEN   make(⟨↓₀⟩); go(⟨↓₀⟩); put(Ty(e_s), Fo(S_{DISTANT.PAST})); go(⟨↑₀⟩);
>   make(⟨↓₁⟩); go(⟨↓₁⟩); put(?Ty(e_s→t)); make(⟨↓₁⟩); go(⟨↓₁⟩);
>   put((Ty(e→(e_s→t), Fo(**W**), ?∃x.Fo(x)); go(⟨↑₁⟩);
>   make(⟨↓₀⟩); go(⟨↓₀⟩); put(?Ty(e))
>   ELSE   abort

In its future tense use, the auxiliary *-rɪ* has an unfixed predicate node (⟨↓*⟩?Ty (e→t)) as its trigger. If this triggering context is present, parsing the auxiliary results in the introduction of a situation argument node which it annotates with the future tense information, as well as building a fixed subject node and a fixed predicate node. The predicate structure that results from parsing the infinitive and the inflected auxiliary is shown in (134) below.

(134)   Parsing: *Jóta*   *a-rɪ*   *maji*   *mpolɪ*
              collect-FV SM1-AUX 6.water later
              'S/he will collect water later'

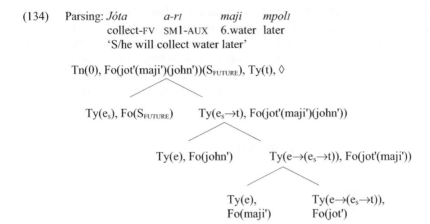

The account presented here captures the future tense interpretation of *-rɪ*, which is here considered to be the result of parsing the auxiliary in the presence of an unfixed predicate node. The lexical entry provided in (133) therefore reflects only this sub-set of lexical actions stemming from parsing *-rɪ*. When the auxiliary is parsed and there is no unfixed predicate node present, the parsing process develops as was seen for the other auxiliary forms in the language, with the auxiliary responsible for the introduction of fixed predicate-argument structure. The past tense use of *-rɪ* employs a past tense prefix which appears before the auxiliary, which is therefore modelled as introducing fixed structure and providing the past tense annotation of the situation argument node – which it also introduces. In its present tense use, it is proposed that in the absence of any specific dedicated tense-aspect marking, the present tense reading is the default interpretation.

6.3. MODELLING THE RANGI AUXILIARY PLACEMENT ALTERNATION

Whilst declarative main clauses exhibit verb-auxiliary order in Rangi, the position of the auxiliary with respect to the verb is inverted in a number of contexts, yielding auxiliary-verb order. The contexts for this inversion are when the auxiliary-based compound construction is:

    (i)   preceded a question word;
    (ii)   part of sentential negation;
    (iii) part of a relative clause;
    (iv) part of a cleft construction; or
    (v)   preceded by a subordinator.

The question here is therefore how best to capture the auxiliary-verb order associated with the future tense in these contexts, and how to model the fact that these constructions exhibit an alternation between pre-verbal and post-verbal auxiliary placement. The proposal developed in Gibson (2012) and Chatzikyriakidis & Gibson (2017) and the one adopted here is that the elements that appear in the left periphery in these contexts are all projected onto an unfixed node. As a result, it is the presence of this unfixed node that enables the auxiliary to be parsed as the next element in the string and which ultimately 'triggers' the auxiliary-verb order. Although the contexts in which the auxiliary-verb order is found vary in terms of their meaning, they are therefore united through the processing strategies involved.

6.3.1. Content questions

A number of previous analyses presented in the DS framework have analysed question words as being projected onto unfixed nodes. This was the account developed by Kempson et al. (2001), Cann et al. (2005), Bouzouita (2008a; 2008b), Chatzikyriakidis (2010) and Gibson (2012) all of which model wh-question words as being projected onto an unfixed node annotated with a type value and a specialised metavariable WH. Parsing content question words was also analysed as introducing a feature Q at the root node indicating the interrogative status of the clause as a whole (Kempson et al. 2001).

Rangi future interrogative phrases which are formed using a wh-expression exhibit auxiliary-infinitive order. This includes both subject and object interrogative phrases, and covers the whole range of content questions. Consider example (135) below.

(135) Ani   á-rɪ   rín-a   ɪ-hɪ   mɪ-ríínga
      who sm1-AUX open-FV DEM-4 4-beehive
      'who will open this beehive?'

The proposal is that parsing *ani* 'who' results in the projection of this element onto an unfixed node. This element also introduces a **WH** metavariable and an interrogative feature Q into the semantic tree (following Bouzouita (2008b) and Chatzikyriakidis (2010)). The metavariable **WH** is a specialised metavariable which is responsible for identifying the question word as interrogative, but which, unlike other metavariables, does not require update to a full formula value before the parse is complete. Formally, the characteristic of **WH** not requiring an update to a fully-specified formula value is captured by the fact that it is not accompanied by the requirement for update (which would be indicated by ?∃x.Fo(x)). The actions induced by parsing *ani* 'who' are captured in the lexical entry outlined in (136) below.[33]

---

[33] Note here that the wh-question word *ani* 'who' is unrestricted in its distribution and can appear either as a subject or as an object in content questions. As such, no case restriction is proposed in the lexical entry.

(136) Lexical entry for the interrogative pronoun *ani* 'who'

> *ani* IF $?Ty(e)$, $\langle\uparrow_0\rangle\langle\uparrow_1{}^*\rangle Ty(t)$
>   THEN $put((\mathbf{WH}_{CLASS1})$, gofirst($?Ty(t))$, $put(Cat(Q))$;
>   ELSE   IF $?Ty(e)$
>   THEN $put((\mathbf{WH}_{CLASS1})$, gofirst($?Ty(t))$, $put(Cat(Q))$;
>   ELSE abort
>   abort

In order for the wh-expression *ani* 'who' to be parsed, the pointer must be at the $?Ty(t)$ root node with no fixed structure present in the tree. If this triggering condition is met, parsing the question word results in the annotation of the root node with the interrogative feature Q and the annotation of the unfixed node. The question word *ani* 'who' can only be used to ask about class 1 (i.e. singular human) nouns. The **WH** metavariable introduced by *ani* 'who' therefore also carries a restriction limiting its possible interpretation to class 1 nouns (indicated by $\mathbf{WH}_{CLASS1}$ in the tree below).[34] The emerging tree is shown in (137) below.

(137) Parsing: *Ani…*

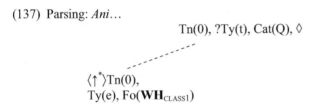

$$Tn(0), ?Ty(t), Cat(Q), \Diamond$$

$$\langle\uparrow^*\rangle Tn(0),$$
$$Ty(e), Fo(\mathbf{WH}_{CLASS1})$$

The analysis presented here assumes that projecting the question word *ani* 'who' onto an unfixed node provides the requisite triggering conditions for parsing the auxiliary. Following the annotation of the unfixed node with the information made available by the wh-expression, the tree can be further developed with content provided by the rest of the clause. The remainder of the tree building process develops in line with the steps that have already been presented for auxiliary constructions above. After the clause-initial wh-expression *ani* 'who' has been projected onto an unfixed node, the auxiliary is parsed and the subject marker *a-* is projected onto a locally unfixed node. The unfixed node introduced by *ani* 'who' and the locally unfixed node introduced by the subject marker can co-exist since they are of different modalities and can be kept distinct in terms of tree logic. The resulting tree is shown in (138) below.

---

[34] In the case of plural human referents, the question word *valani* 'who (plural)' is used and possible substituents for *valani* would subsequently be restricted to class 2 (which encodes plural human noun) – and would be indicated by the restricted metavariable $\mathbf{WH}_{CLASS2}$.

(138) Parsing: *Ani a-...*

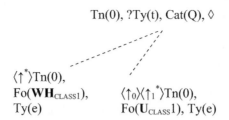

$$Tn(0), ?Ty(t), Cat(Q), \Diamond$$

$\langle\uparrow^*\rangle Tn(0),$
$Fo(\mathbf{WH}_{CLASS1}),$
$Ty(e)$

$\langle\uparrow_0\rangle\langle\uparrow_1^*\rangle Tn(0),$
$Fo(\mathbf{U}_{CLASS}1), Ty(e)$

Parsing the auxiliary form introduces the first fixed structure into the tree and enables the fixing of the tree node addresses of the previously underspecified nodes. Parsing the infinitive after the auxiliary results in the same steps as were presented for parsing the more Bantu-typical auxiliary-verb order in Section 5.1, with the fixed structure collapsing with the structure introduced by the auxiliary. The only difference between the Rangi future tense auxiliary-verb constructions and those presented for Swahili is that in Rangi the verb is in the infinitival form meaning that it does not host a subject marker.

Gibson (2012) proposes that infinitives are always parsed on an unfixed node. However, a different approach was taken in Chatzikyriakidis and Gibson (2017) in which it was assumed that it is only in the verb-auxiliary order that the infinitive is projected onto an unfixed node. In contrast, when the auxiliary appears before the verb, the infinitive can be associated with a fixed tree node address as soon as it is parsed. This account fits with the DS approach in which variant word orders are considered to stem from differences in the processing strategies employed when different words are encountered. The differences in processing strategies are the result of different computational actions being applied or are explicitly encoded in the lexical entries of the words (or morphemes) that are encountered. The assumption here is therefore that when the infinitive appears first, it can be viewed as 'fronted' to a certain extent and therefore as behaving in a way similar to other fronted elements which appear at the left periphery – as has been seen in this section to be the case for question words for example.

Additional support for this account also comes from the variation found within interrogative constructions. Whilst content questions exhibit pre-verbal auxiliary placement, the order verb-auxiliary is found in polar interrogatives. Consider examples (139) and (140) below where the infinitive still appears before the auxiliary despite the interrogative status of the sentence.

(139) Dóm-a   mw-íise   úʊ?
       go-FV   SM2pl-AUX.FUT   Q
       'Will you (pl) go?' (Rangi, Gibson 2012: 113)

(140) Haánd-a   w-íise   vi-ryo   ʊ-hʊ   mw-ááka   ʊ́ʊ?
       plant-FV   SM2sg-AUX   8-millet DEM-3   3-year   Q
       'Will you plant millet this year?' (Rangi, Gibson 2012: 113)

The claim here is that in interrogative utterances which do not have sentence initial content words (such as those shown above), the parse proceeds in the same manner as for declarative utterances: the infinitive is projected onto an unfixed node and the auxiliary subsequently enables the fixing of this node through the introduction of fixed predicate argument structure. This all happens before the interrogative marker ʊ́ʊ comes into parse. In this way, it is not the interrogative status of the clause which yields auxiliary-verb order but rather the processing strategy employed. In polar interrogatives, there is no element at the left periphery to enable the auxiliary to be parsed as the next element and verb-auxiliary order is therefore found.

This observation resembles that made by Bouzouita & Chatzikyriakidis (2009: 194) who note that the Person Case Constraint (PPC) – a restriction which prohibits the co-occurrence of certain clitics – seems not to be semantic (as it may at first appear) but can rather be explained as a processing constraint which stems from the prohibition of more than one unfixed node at any given time (see also Chapter 7). Thus, word order variation patterns, such as those found in Rangi interrogatives, are not determined by the interrogative nature of the clause but rather by the processing strategy employed.

A crucial element of the proposal made in Gibson (2012) for Rangi auxiliary constructions, as well as in Bouzouita (2008b) for clitic placement in Medieval Spanish and Chatzikyriakidis (2010) for clitic placement in varieties of Modern Greek, is that the unfixed node trigger that is seen in one context (for example, in content questions in Rangi) can be generalised out to all contexts in which this word order alternation (or clitic placement) is found. This is demonstrated for Rangi in the remainder of this chapter which shows that the verb-auxiliary order is triggered by the presence of an unfixed node as part of the processing strategy in sentential negation, relative and subordinate clauses and cleft constructions.

6.3.2. *Sentential negation*

Sentential negation is achieved in Rangi through the presence of the negative marker *sí* which appears before the verb phrase and the negative polarity item *tʊkʊ*, which appears either after the verb or clause-finally.

(141) Sí   tú-rɪ   rɪm-a   ɪ-rɪ   i-yʊʊnda   tʊkʊ
       NEG SM1pl-AUX   farm-FV DEM-5   5-farm   NEG
       'we will not dig this farm'

(142) Sí   ndí-rɪ   dom-a na   Kondoa   tʊkʊ
       NEG SM1sg-AUX   go-FV CONN Kondoa   NEG
       'I will not go to Kondoa'

As can be seen in the examples above, negative future tense constructions exhibit auxiliary-verb order. The analysis developed here is that the negative marker *sí* is projected onto an unfixed predicate node, reflecting its underspecified position within the tree when it is parsed as the first element in the clause, and thereby giving rise to the auxiliary-verb order. The steps of this process are laid out below, drawing on the sentence in (142) above.

The negative form *sí* has an unfixed predicate node as its lexical trigger. In instances in which *sí* functions as part of a bipartite negative construction, the only contribution it makes to the clause is to encode negative polarity. However, *sí* also functions as a negative copula where it is the predicative base of a negative clause. As such, the proposal here is that *sí* can be modelled as introducing the metavariable formula **BE** (following the account provided by Cann (2006, 2007) for English auxiliaries). The lexical entry for the negative marker *sí* is shown in (143) below.

(143) Lexical entry for the negative marker *sí*

$sí$ IF $?Ty(t)$, $\langle\downarrow*\rangle?Ty(e{\rightarrow}t)$
     THEN $put(Pol(Neg))$; $go(\langle\downarrow*\rangle)$; $make(\langle\downarrow_0\rangle)$; $go(\langle\downarrow_0\rangle)$; $put(?e_s)$;
           $go(\langle\uparrow_0\rangle)$; $make(\langle\downarrow_1\rangle)$; $go(\langle\downarrow_1\rangle)$; $put(Ty(e{\rightarrow}t), Fo(\mathbf{BE}))$;
           $go(\langle\uparrow\rangle)$; $make(\langle\downarrow_0\rangle)$; $go(\langle\downarrow_0\rangle)$; $put(?Ty(e)$; $go(\langle\uparrow_0\rangle)$; $go(\langle\uparrow_1\rangle)$;
           . . .
     ELSE   abort

The actions encoded by *sí* result in the annotation of the root node with Pol(Neg)). Parsing *sí* also induces the construction of a situation argument node and a predicate node with the annotation Fo(**BE**). The metavariable **BE** serves as a placeholder in the same way as other metavariable values. However, it can be enriched by information from a variety of elements. In the case of its use as a negative copula, **BE** can receive interpretation from an adjectival element. However, in the case of a negative construction **BE** can also be updated by full predicate formula from a verb.

(144) Parsing: *Sí* ...

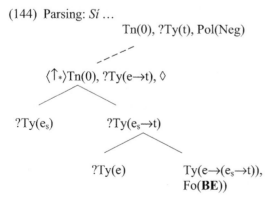

Once the negative marker has been parsed, the remainder of the verbal complex is processed following the steps that have been outlined so far. Parsing the auxiliary introduces fixed predicate-argument structure, thereby enabling the update of the unfixed node to a fully-specified fixed tree address. The subject marker on the auxiliary is identified with a referent (provided either by an overt subject expression or from the context). It is also proposed that parsing the auxiliary in the presence of the unfixed predicate node introduces the future tense interpretation – which is captured on the situation argument node. The verb contributes the lexico-semantic information to the clause, providing update for the **BE** metavariable. Following Marten (2002), it is assumed that the prepositional phrase *na Kondoa* 'to Kondoa' is of type-*e* and can fulfil the requirement on the object node. The negative marker *tʋkʋ* is considered to make no contribution to the structure building process, rather it encodes negative polarity. In sentential negation, the negative marker *sí* has already introduced the negative encoding into the clause so *tʋkʋ* merely reiterates (and re-decorates) this information. However, in certain contexts *tʋkʋ* can be the sole marker of negation in a clause (this is discussed further below). A snapshot of the final stage of the derivation is shown in (145) below.

(145) Parsing: *Sí ndírı doma na Kondoa tʋkʋ* 'I will not go to Kondoa'

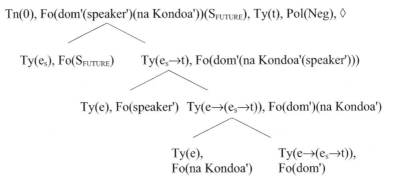

The unfixed node analysis is further supported by the presence of examples in Rangi in which negation is marked solely through the use of the negative polarity item *tʋkʋ*. Crucially, when negation is marked by *tʋkʋ* alone – in negative infinitive, prohibitive and in non-verbal predication constructions – the auxiliary-verb order is not triggered. This can be seen in the prohibitive construction in (146) below.

(146) Sínj-a   tú-rı   mbúri tʋkʋ.
       slaughter-FV SM1pl-AUX   9.goat NEG
       'We should not slaughter the goat' lit. 'We are not to slaughter the goat'

In such instances, *tuku* can be considered responsible for decorating the root node with the negative annotation. But since the negative marker *sí* does not appear before the verbal complex, there is no unfixed predicate node present and the auxiliary is not licensed to be parsed. The verb-auxiliary structure is therefore found. The tree building process proceeds in the same way as was presented for declarative main clauses – i.e. with the infinitive being projected onto an unfixed predicate node and the auxiliary inducing fixed structure. This is analogous to what was seen in Section 6.3.1 above which attributed the differences in auxiliary placement in content interrogatives and polar interrogatives to the different processing strategies involved.

6.3.3. *Relative clauses*

Future tense relative clause constructions in Rangi also result in pre-verbal auxiliary placement. There are two strategies for the formation of relative clauses in Rangi: one employs the relative pronoun *-eene* which shows agreement with the relative head. This can be seen in examples (147) and (148) below. In the second strategy, there is no overt relative pronoun and the relative is encoded by the presence of a high tone subject marker (149). In both instances however, the auxiliary appears pre-verbally in future tense constructions.

(147) Ku-untu kw-eene ndı-rı   dóm-a ...
       16-place 16-REL   SM1sg-AUX go-FV
       'the place where I will go...' (Oliver Stegen p.c.)

(148) Mwaarimu mw-eene a-rı   lok-a   a-boh-a
       1-teacher   1-REL   SM1-AUX   go-FV   SM1-be.good-FV
       'the teacher who will leave is good' (Gibson 2012: 118)

(149) Mu-lay-ır-a   ha-antu á-rı   rím-a   isiku.
       OM1-show-APPL-FV   16-place SM1-AUX   farm-FV 9.today
       'show him/her the place where s/he will farm today.
       (Gibson 2012: 118)

Relative clauses have been modelled in Dynamic Syntax as a conjunction of two trees connected by the presence of a shared term (Kempson et al. 2011; Cann et al. 2005b). Specifically, the rule of LINK ADJUNCTION (FOR RELATIVES) (Cann et al. 2005b: 88) induces the building of a type-e node to a new type-t node. The LINK ADJUNCTION RULE introduces a requirement that the LINKED structure contains a copy of the formula value of the head noun. This stipulation is captured formally by the introduction of the requirement for a copy of the formula value i.e. Fo(α) to be present somewhere in the eventual tree, as indicated by $?\langle \downarrow_* \rangle$Fo($\alpha$), which holds at the root node in the LINKED tree. This copy of the head noun is often introduced through a pronominal element within the relative clause – possibly a relative pronoun or a resumptive pronoun (see Kula & Marten 2011). After the application of the rule of LINK ADJUNCTION FOR RELATIVES, the LINKed tree can be further developed through information made available by the relative clause. After the relative clause has been parsed, the main tree is developed further with information provided by the matrix clause.

Following the DS analyses of relative clauses and previous DS analyses of relative clauses in Bantu languages, Rangi relative clauses are modelled using two trees constructed in parallel and connected via a LINK relation. Under this approach, the relativiser is responsible for the transition which licenses the closure of one incomplete structure and the opening up of another (in the vein of Kempson and Wei 2017). Crucially, the account developed here employs an unfixed node for parsing relative clauses in Rangi, meaning that the presence of the auxiliary-verb order in these constructions fits with the emerging generalisation that all constructions in which the auxiliary-verb order is found in the future tense are associated with the presence of an unfixed node as part of the processing strategy. In the case of a relative clause, this unfixed node is projected from the LINKed tree which is being constructed in parallel to the main tree. This unfixed node is annotated with the copy of the subject expression *mwaarimʊ* 'teacher', as can be seen below.

(150)   Parsing: *Mwaarimʊ mweene…* 'The teacher who…'

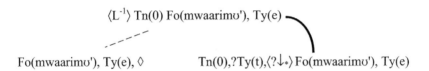

$\langle L^{-1} \rangle$ Tn(0) Fo(mwaarimʊ'), Ty(e)

Fo(mwaarimʊ'), Ty(e), ◊   Tn(0),?Ty(t),$\langle ?\downarrow_* \rangle$ Fo(mwaarimʊ'), Ty(e)

The parse proceeds with the information provided by the relative clause. The LINKed tree is built through a combination of computational rules and lexical input. Parsing the auxiliary introduces the first fixed structure in the tree. This enables the fixing of the head noun as the logical subject of the clause, as well as satisfying the requirement that the copy of the head noun is found somewhere in the tree before the parse is complete.

In terms of being able to account for both relativisation strategies, the proposal is that parsing the relativiser *-eene* licenses the launch of a LINK transition from the type-*e* node (the head noun) which is already present in the tree to a new type-*t*-requiring node in a parallel emergent tree. The relativiser is also assumed to be responsible for the provision of the copy of this head noun. Since there is no fixed structure present in the tree at this initial stage of structure-building, the copy of the head noun is projected onto an unfixed node. In the future tense construction, the presence of this unfixed node is therefore considered to be responsible for pre-verbal auxiliary placement. It is also assumed that in contexts in which the relative pronoun is not present, the same lexical actions are induced by way of a process of pragmatic enrichment in the sense described by McCormack (2008), which argues for the pragmatic existence of constructive case in Bantu. This is also the case for English relative clauses which are formed without relative pronouns, e.g. *The food I most like to eat is stew* (see Cann et al. 2005b).

6.3.4. *Cleft constructions*

Cleft structures are formed in Rangi using the copula *nɪ*, which appears before the fronted element – typically a nominal expression. An example of this can be seen in (151) below.

(151) Ní   nɪ́ɪnɪ   ndí-rɪ   kán-y-a   ʊ-hʊ   mʊ-tɪ
      COP 1sg.PP SM1sg-AUX fall-CAUS-FV DEM-3 3-tree
      'it is me, I will fell this tree'

The Dynamic Syntax framework makes available two strategies for parsing cleft constructions. As focus constructions, the left-dislocated elements in cleft constructions have been modelled, like wh-expressions, as decorating unfixed nodes (Kempson et al. 2001: 150–89; Cann et al. 2005b: 153–4). The observation that certain types of cleft structures involve a presentational or backgrounding effect however, means that they have also been represented through the construction of a pair of LINKed trees (Kempson et al. 2011b). Under a LINK structure analysis, the 'clefted' element decorates a Ty(e) node connected to the main tree by a LINK relation (see Kempson et al. 2011 for the use of this strategy in siSwati). This strategy also reflects the observed cross-linguistic parallels between cleft constructions and relative clauses.

Following on from previous analyses of cleft structures within DS, and the observed parallels between cleft structures and relative clauses, an account is developed here in which the left-dislocated element in Rangi cleft structures is related to the main tree via a LINK structure. This LINK structure is used to capture the pragmatic impact of clefting the nominal expression and the contrastive focus interpretation that ensues. Parsing the copula at the left periphery and the obligatory expression that follows it are analysed as resulting in the establishment of basic skeletal predicate-argument structure and the launch of a LINK relation from the ?Ty(e) node and from the ?Ty(e) node. The transition to a type-t-requiring node in a parallel tree, also imposes the requirement for a term to be shared by the LINKed tree and the main tree once it has been constructed. In this way, the LINK relation ensures the flow of information between the two trees which is achieved via the presence of a shared term.

The proposal for Rangi clefts is that parsing the clause-initial *nɪ* and the clefted nominal element induces a LINK structure. Adopting a LINK analysis of

Rangi cleft structures is in line with the LINK structure analysis proposed for clefts in siSwati (Kempson et al. 2011b) and for Japanese (Seraku 2013a). However, for Rangi it is also proposed that parsing *nɪ* also results in the introduction of an unfixed node as part of this LINKed tree. The emerging tree is shown in (152) below.

(152) Parsing: *Nɪ...*

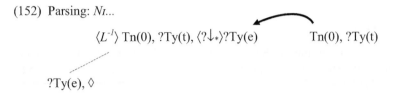

$\langle L^{-1} \rangle$ Tn(0), ?Ty(t), $\langle ?\downarrow_* \rangle$?Ty(e)   Tn(0), ?Ty(t)

?Ty(e), ◊

The remaining structure is parsed following the steps that have been laid out for the auxiliary constructions more broadly, with the auxiliary introducing fixed structure and the main verb providing update to a full formula value for the predicate node.

6.3.5. *Subordinate clauses*

The final context in which the auxiliary-verb order is found in Rangi future tense construction is with subordinate clauses (153).

(153) N-íyó-wás-a   j00lɪ ndí-rɪ   rih-a   ada.
      SM1sg-PROG-think-FV how SM1sg-AUX pay-FV 10.fees
      'I am thinking about how I will pay the fees.' (Rangi, Gibson 2012: 121)

The proposal is that the pre-verbal placement of the auxiliary found in Rangi subordinate clauses can also be captured by reference to the unfixed node trigger adopted throughout this section. Subordinate clauses in Rangi are commonly introduced by an overt morphological subordinator. Following the account proposed by Chatzikyriakidis & Gibson (2017), subordinators in Rangi are taken here as projecting an unfixed node which provides the necessary triggering conditions for parsing the auxiliary – thereby yielding the auxiliary-verb order.

Under such an account, parsing the subordinator *jooIɪ* 'how' results in the launch of a LINK relation (as was also proposed to be the case in conditional structures involving the English conditional conjunction *if* (Gregoromichelaki 2006) and the projection of an unfixed situation argument node. This unfixed situation argument node reflects the requirement for there to be a new situation node in the subordinate clause. Following the parse of *jooIɪ* 'how', the following tree state emerges.

(154) Parsing: *Níyówása joolɪ...* 'I am wondering how...'

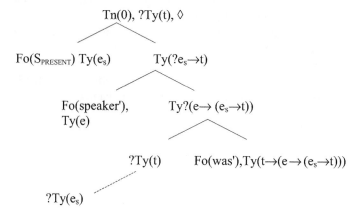

Since the parse of subordinate clauses also involves an unfixed node, the generalisation that the auxiliary-verb order is found in future tense constructions which involve an unfixed node as part of the processing strategy can be maintained. In the case of content questions, this is an unfixed node annotated with the **WH** metavariable, with sentential negation this is an unfixed predicate node, whilst in relative clauses and cleft constructions the unfixed node is projected from the parallel LINKed tree and in subordinate clauses the unfixed node is an unfixed predicate node.

6.4. SUMMARY

The analysis presented in the current chapter provides an exploration of some of the key tools and concepts on which the Dynamic Syntax framework is based. It shows the steps involved in the incremental establishment of propositional structure in a similar way to that which has been shown throughout the book so far. It builds on previous accounts which have been developed within the framework. Cann (2011) for example, developed an account of auxiliary verbs in English under which the interpretation of auxiliary strings can be captured in a compositional and dynamic way. The structure which is introduced is underspecified but its interpretation is restricted enough to ensure the appropriate interpretation, with the structure introduced by the main verb collapsing with that which has previously been introduced by the auxiliary.

The discussion presented in this chapter has also provided a case study which exemplifies the predictive nature of Dynamic Syntax. The framework is capable of capturing the unfolding of tree structure in the Bantu clauses, it is also able to capture the way in which the specific elements combine across a compound verbal construction – as is seen in auxiliary constructions in Rangi (and Bantu more broadly). However, the way in which the word order alternation in Rangi can be seen to stem from the natural tree logic employed by Dynamic Syntax, further confirms the status of the framework as a grammar formalism, rather than as merely a parsing device. Not only can the DS approach naturally capture the alternation between pre and post-verbal auxiliary placement in Rangi, this alternation is in fact predicted on the basis of the unfixed node constraint. The implications of this and the parallels between the observations for Rangi and other unrelated languages is the focus of the next chapter.

7

CROSS-LINGUISTIC PARALLELS: PARSING DYNAMICS BEYOND BANTU

Within the Dynamic Syntax perspective, lexical entries are considered to be language-specific. However, the transition rules and the basic mechanisms of the framework are considered to be universally available. As the empirical coverage of the DS approach expands, cross-linguistic parallels can be more closely examined, often as a result of in-depth explorations of a given phenomenon in a single language. One of the observations that results from this growing empirical coverage is that distinct phenomena in unrelated languages are often modelled using similar parsing/processing strategies. This chapter explores to what extent the central issues raised and the properties of the theoretical approach observed in the book so far can be applied outside of the Bantu family.

The chapter explores cross-linguistic manifestations of the constraint on underspecification – namely the prohibition of the co-occurrence of multiple unfixed nodes in the tree building process. The chapter does not propose new formal accounts of these phenomena, but rather draws on previous accounts that revolve around this restriction. Specifically, it examines the ways in which this is manifested in Romance languages and varieties of Modern Greek (in relation to clitic placement), Japanese and Korean (in relation to word order phenomena), and Bantu languages (in terms of double object constructions). In doing so, it seeks to highlight parallels in the incremental dynamic parsing process with those developed in relation to the Bantu languages. This section also situates the account proposed for Rangi which relies centrally on the Unique Unfixed Node Constraint in a broader typological perspective.

7.1. CONSTRAINING UNDERSPECIFICATION: THE UNIQUE UNFIXED NODE CONSTRAINT

There is a constraint operative in the Dynamic Syntax approach that prohibits the co-existence of more than one unfixed node of the same modality at any point in the tree building process. This constraint follows directly from the Logic of Finite Trees under which two unfixed nodes of the same modality cannot be kept distinct. The first introduction of explicit terminology to refer to this restriction (although not the first application of the constraint) appeared in Seraku (2013a) where the term the Unique Unfixed Node Constraint was coined and defined as in (155) below.

(155) The Unique Unfixed Node Constraint (Seraku 2013a: 210)

> Under the Logic of Finite Trees two unfixed tree nodes of the same modality will necessarily collapse on to each other

This constraint played a central role in the account of auxiliary placement in Rangi that was presented in Chapter 6. A brief outline of the analysis will be presented here before a discussion of the way in which this constraint can be seen to be operative in a number of other phenomena and languages.

Certain auxiliary-based constructions in the Tanzania Bantu language Rangi exhibit a word order alternation in which the auxiliary appears after the verb in main clause declarative contexts but appears before the verb in negation, subordinate clauses, and content questions. Although this verb-auxiliary order is typologically unusual, the main consideration in the Dynamic Syntax approach is how to capture this alternation in formal terms. It has been proposed that in the verb-auxiliary order, the verb is projected onto an unfixed predicate node and that first instance of fixed structure is introduced into the tree once the auxiliary is accessed (see Chapter 6; Gibson 2012; Chatzikyriakidis & Gibson 2017). The contexts in which the auxiliary appears before the verb all involve the presence of an unfixed node as part of the processing strategy. The DS approach has commonly used the projection of an unfixed node to model relative clauses and content-questions. The proposal is that with the clause-initial element already projected onto an unfixed node, it is not possible to introduce another unfixed node since this would lead to the co-occurrence of two unfixed nodes of the same modality. Rather, the presence of the left-peripheral elements (question words or relative clause markers for example) provide the requisite triggering conditions for the auxiliary to be parsed as the next element. This then gives rise to the auxiliary-verb order with which these constructions are associated.

It is important to note that the restriction on two unfixed nodes is not a stipulation or a formal 'rule' in the Dynamic Syntax system. Rather it is a result of the tree logic (as provided by the Logic of Finite Tress defined by Blackburn & Meyer-Viol 1994) which means that the two unfixed nodes have an identical tree node address and therefore cannot be kept distinct. In other words, the putative 'two' nodes are in fact one and the same node and will necessarily collapse onto each other. It is important to note, however, that two unfixed nodes decorated with different locality restrictions can co-exist. That is, a locally unfixed node and an unfixed node can both be present in the tree since they have tree node addresses that are defined in distinct terms from the root node ($\langle\uparrow_0\rangle\langle\uparrow_1{}^*\rangle Tn(n)$ and $\langle\uparrow^*\rangle Tn(n)$, respectively).

Recourse to the Unique Unfixed Node Constraint accurately captures the ordering restrictions exhibited by auxiliary placement in Rangi. The question is then whether there are reflexes of the same constraint operative elsewhere, possibly resulting in different effects in different languages.[36] Indeed, a range of work shows the effects of this constraint cross-linguistically in the so-called Person Case Constraint (Chatzikyriakidis & Kempson 2011), clitic placement in various varieties of Modern Greek (Chatzikyriakidis 2009; 2010), and in different historical stages of Spanish (Bouzouita 2008b), as well as the interaction between scrambling and constructive case in Korean and Japanese (Kempson & Kiaer 2010), the properties and interpretation of clefts in Japanese (Seraku 2013a; 2013b), as well as object marking restrictions in Bantu more broadly (Kempson et al. 2013).

7.1.1. *Clitic placement in Medieval Spanish and Modern Greek*

Clitic placement in Medieval Spanish exhibits an alternation between the pre-verbal position and post-verbal position. Whilst in non-root clauses proclisis dominates, enclisis is found in root clause contexts. However, despite this general pattern, in some syntactic environments only proclisis is possible. These contexts include root clauses in which a: (i) wh-element; (ii) negative adverb; (iii) non-coreferential complement; or (iv) prepositional or a predicative complement appears at the left-periphery, as described by Bouzouita (2007; 2008a; 2008b).[37]

Bouzouita (2008a; 2008b) provides a characterisation of this patterning by employing the tools of the Dynamic Syntax approach under which accusative clitics in Medieval Spanish are seen to have two possible triggering contexts in their lexical entry: preverbal clitics are constructed from a type-t-requiring node, whilst post-verbal clitics have a type-e-requiring node as their lexical trigger. Moreover, parsing the proclitic is associated with the presence of: (i) a negative marker; (ii) an unfixed node; and (iii) a tense requirement on the ?Ty(t) node. In contrast, enclitics have no such triggers (Bouzouita 2008b: 302).

The observation that is particularly relevant here is the proposal of an unfixed node as a trigger for the pre-verbal placement of the clitic. The contexts that trigger proclisis can also be seen to be remarkably similar to those with which pre-verbal auxiliary placement is associated in Rangi: i.e. content questions in both languages, (certain types of) negation in both languages, and the more general presence of some element at the left periphery (in Rangi this was shown to include fronted constituents, whilst in Medieval Spanish this includes predicative complements). Therefore, not only are there parallels in terms of the formal representation of the triggering conditions, but also in the contexts in which the alternation occurs from a descriptive perspective. In this way, the

---

[36] This is a question which was also previously raised in Kempson et al. (2008). Credit is also owed to Ruth Kempson for a great deal of discussion on this point over the years.

[37] A similar account of the general patterns observed in relation to the Person Case Constraint (PCC) is also proposed, where the PCC is argued to be no more than a restriction on underspecification – a hard-wired constraint of the tree-logic language underpinning the Dynamic Syntax framework – rather than a language-specific idiosyncrasy.

restriction on the co-occurrence of unfixed nodes of the same modality can be seen to play a role in the clitic placement alternation in Medieval Spanish.

A similar situation holds for varieties of Modern Greek. The Greek systems can be divided into two broad types: there are those varieties in which clitics generally precede the verb in non-imperative finite forms and, in contrast, immediately follow the verb in imperatives, gerunds and infinitives. Standard Modern Greek, for example, falls into this category. The second type of variety is that in which clitics immediately follow the verb except when one of a number of elements appears at the left periphery. Cypriot Greek falls into this latter category.

Chatzikyriakidis (2010) examines four varieties of Modern Greek and proposes that clitic placement in these varieties is intimately connected to the associated processing strategies. Clitics in Cypriot Greek for example, generally appear as enclitics – i.e. after the verb (as was also seen in Chapter 6). However, when one of a number of left peripheral elements is present in the clause, they appear as proclitics. Crucially for the current discussion, these functional elements and the contexts with which they are associated are wh-elements, a number of tense and modality markers (including subjunctive markers, negative particles and the future particle), focused constituents and subordinating conjunctions.

The account developed by Chatzikyriakidis (2010) is based on the idea that the rule of *ADJUNCTION (which was also employed in Medieval Spanish, Bouzouita 2002; 2008a; 2008b) can serve as a basis for a generalised proclitic trigger in Cypriot Greek. The development of Cypriot Greek is therefore thought to have involved fronted elements, such as subjects, objects, prepositional phrases, adverbs and wh-elements, all of which are associated with an unfixed node as part of their processing strategy. Pronouns have been noted to have a tendency to appear early in the sentence – the suggestion being that this minimises the cognitive effort involved in the search for identification of the pronoun (Cann & Kempson 2008). One of the effects of this is that (pronominal) clitics appear as soon as possible in the relevant domain – in other words, they appear preverbally. In an earlier stage of the development of the language, this would have just been a tendency regulated by the pragmatic considerations with which the fronted elements were associated. However, over time, the presence of different elements signalled the emergent domain which was projected onto unfixed nodes, and the tendency of these clitics to appear as early as possible resulted in the encoding of the unfixed node strategy as a trigger for parsing the clitic.[38] A further restriction meant that enclisis occurred in the absence of any of the proclisis-inducing environments. Again, the adoption of the unfixed node as a parsing trigger and the absence of this trigger for enclisis closely mirrors the analysis developed for Rangi. It seems to be another reflex of the restriction on the co-occurrence of multiple unfixed nodes at play: if there is already an unfixed node present onto which the fronted element is projected, a second unfixed node

---

[38] See also Chatzikyriakidis & Gibson (2017) for more on the routinisation which is assumed to have been involved in this process.

cannot be induced onto which the clitic could be projected. As a result, the verb is parsed before the clitic, resulting in enclisis.

7.1.2. Cleft constructions and multiple foci in Japanese

The presence of two types of clefts in Japanese, along with their distinct syntactic behaviour, has been widely observed (Kuroda 2005; Cho et al. 2008; Hiraiwa & Ishihara 2011, Seraku 2013a; 2013b). These two types of clefts in Japanese are distinguished by the presence versus absence of a case marker. In clefts with multiple foci, the first focused element must be case-marked and the second element can appear in a non-case-marked form. For the purposes of the discussion here, the terminology adopted by Seraku (2013b) is employed: cleft that hosts a case marker are referred to as clefts$_{+C}$ whilst those that appear without the case marker are termed clefts$_{C-}$. Seraku (2013b) examines multiple foci in Japanese clefts and claims that while the facts associated with clefts and multiple foci in Japanese may provide a challenge for mainstream generative approaches, the DS approach can naturally node model – and predict – the distribution of case markers in these cleft constructions.

The proposal is that the focused (nominal) elements annotate unfixed nodes introduced by the rule of LOCAL *ADJUNCTION. In the case of clefts$_{+C}$ constructions, the tree node of this element can be updated to a fully-specified fixed tree node address when the nominative case marker -ga is parsed. This serves to resolve the unfixed node as the subject node following the account of constructive case that has been employed on a number of occasions in DS (Kempson & Chatzikyriakidis 2009; Chatzikyriakidis 2010; Seraku 2013a). In clefts$_{C-}$ constructions however, since there is no case marker, the address of the unfixed node is resolved by the general rule of UNIFICATION, as the unfixed node decorated with the nominal unifies with the fixed Ty(e) node annotated with the metavariable. A similar account is developed for modelling cleft constructions with multiple foci. However, crucially, this analysis hinges on the Unique Unified Node Constraint, which, it is argued, can be used to account for the facts associated with multiple foci in Japanese clefts.

In Japanese clefts, more than one element can be focal. Consider the example in (156) below in which both *Tom* and *Mary* are focused constituents.

(156) purezento-o age-ta   no-wa Tom-ga Mary-ni da
      present-ACC give-PAST NO-TOP Tom-NOM Mary-DAT COP
      'it is TOM to MARY that gave a present.' (Japanese, Seraku 2013b: 165)

The analysis proposed by Seraku (2013b) is that a focused nominal is parsed on a locally unfixed node. For the sentence in (156), following the parse of *no-wa*, the rule of LOCAL *ADJUNCTION induces a locally unfixed node onto which the first focused element – *Tom* – is parsed. The nominal *Tom* is marked with the nominative case particle -*ga,* meaning that it can immediately be fixed as the subject and receives a fixed tree node address at the subject node. There are no unfixed nodes present at this point in the tree, meaning that the rule of LOCAL *ADJUNCTION can apply again, inducing another locally unfixed node. This is also a crucial consideration in the application of the Unique Unified Node Constraint. Whilst no two unfixed nodes of the same modality can co-exist, as soon as the tree node address of the first unfixed node has been updated to a fully-specified fixed tree node address, another unfixed node can be introduced into the structure, either through the application of the rule of LOCAL * ADJUNCTION or through the lexical actions encoded in a lexical entry. This is what happens in the case of Japanese clefts. Following the fixing of the tree node address of the argument *Tom*, the second focused constituent *Mary* can also be parsed on a locally unfixed node. This unfixed node is resolved when the dative marker –*ni* is parsed.

The copula *da* which appears at the end of the cleft introduces a propositional metavariable (consistent with the analysis provided by Cann et al. (2005b) and Cann (2006, 2007)). However, since Japanese is a head-final language, parsing the copula allows the reiteration of any actions that have already been contributed by the wider context, including actions encoded in the verb (in the example above *age* 'give'). This re-firing of the actions encoded by the verb subsequently allows the fleshing out of the propositional structure, where the focused nominals (*Tom* and *Mary*) have already been incorporated.

Such an account can be developed for clefts$_{+C}$ construction in example (156) above since both focused nominal forms are case-marked. Consider however, the clefts$_{C-}$ examples below in which the case marking varies. (Data from Seraku 2013b: 166, 167).

(157) *purezento-o age-ta   no-wa Tom Mary da.
       present-ACC give-PAST NO-TOP Tom Mary COP
       Int. 'It is TOM to MARY that gave a present'

(158) *purezento-o age-ta   no-wa Tom Mary-ni   da.
       present-ACC give-PAST NO-TOP Tom Mary-DAT COP
       Int. 'It is TOM to MARY that gave a present'

(159) purezento-o age-ta   no-wa Tom-ga$_i$ Mary$_j$ da.
       present-ACC give-PAST NO-TOP Tom-NOM Mary COP
       'it is TOM to MARY that gave a present'

Following on from the account described above, Seraku (2013b) argues that the variation in grammaticality that can be seen in examples (157) to (159) above can be accounted for on the basis of the unfixed node analysis of focused nominals in clefts. Specifically, example (157) is ungrammatical since neither *Tom* nor *Mary* are case-marked. As such, an unfixed node for the first focused nominal cannot be fixed before the second nominal is encountered. Similarly, example (158) is ungrammatical because the first noun *Tom* is not case marked. There is therefore no way to fix the tree node address of the locally unfixed node onto which it is projected. When *Mary* is parsed, this is also projected onto a locally unfixed node, which results in the presence of two inconsistent annotations on this unfixed node and the parse fails. In contrast, example (159) is grammatical since only one of the focused nominals is case-marked (as was also seen in the ungrammatical example (158)). The first nominal hosts the nominative case marker *-ga*, meaning that by the time the second focused element is encountered the first unfixed node has already received a fixed tree node address and *Mary* can be projected onto a locally unfixed node.

A final observation can also be made, and this follows naturally from the tree logic. In Japanese, it is also possible to have more than two focal elements in a clause. However, this is only possible if the forms appear with the appropriate case marking patterns. In descriptive terms this means that either; (i) all three nominals must be case marked; or (ii) the first two nominals must be case-marked but the last form can appear without a case marker. In DS terms, this patterning restriction can be accounted for by reference to the analysis outlined above where the unfixed node receives a fixed tree node address as a result of the case marker being parsed. This means that only the final focal element can be unmarked, since this is not followed by another unfixed node projection. This is exactly what is seen in the language.

(160) age-ta   no-wa Tom-ga   Mary-n   purezento-o da.
give-PAST NO-TOP Tom-NOM Mary-DAT present-ACC COP
'it is TOM to MARY a PRESENT that gave'

In this way, the restriction on the co-occurrence of multiple unfixed nodes of the same modality (Unique Unfixed Node Constraint) can be seen to accurately capture the otherwise seemingly idiosyncratic case marking properties of multiple foci constructions in Japanese. The presence versus absence of the case marker relates directly to the ability of the unfixed node to receive a fixed tree node address at a crucial stage in the unfolding of the partial trees, and therefore for the parse to proceed. As will be seen below, this constraint has also been used to account for long distance scrambling effects in Japanese (Kempson & Kiaer 2009; 2010).

7.1.3. *Multiple object marking in Bantu*

Reference has also been made to the Unique Unfixed Node Constraint in accounts of object marking in Bantu languages. In addition to exhibiting agreement with subjects, Bantu languages regularly exhibit agreement in which object arguments are cross-referenced on the verb. Using the DS approach, Bantu object markers are projected onto a locally unfixed node, which is subsequently annotated with information encoded in the noun class of the marker in question, thereby restricting the possible substituents for the referent (see Chapter 3 for additional details). The projection of object arguments onto locally unfixed nodes is also used explain that in many Bantu languages, multiple object markers cannot co-occur.

The exact properties of Bantu object marking vary between languages. As is the case in many Bantu languages, Herero exhibits subject and object agreement that appear through the presence of subject and object markers in the verbal template. In Herero, an object marker can cross-reference either a direct or an indirect object. However, only one object marker can appear in a given verb form, although it can refer to either the direct or indirect object.

(161) Ú-térék-èr-à   òvá-éndà ònyàmà p-òngàndà
      SM1-cook-APPL-FV 2-guests 9.meat 16-9.house
      's/he cooks meat for the guests at home.'

(162) ù-vé-térék-èr-a   ònyámà p-òngàndà
      SM1-OM2-cook-APPL-FV 9.meat 16-9.house
      's/he cooks them meat at home.'

(163) ú-í-térék-èr-à   òvá-éndà p-òngàndà
      SM1-OM9-cook-APPL-FV 2-guests 16-9.house
      's/he cooks it for the guests at the house.'

(164) *ú-vé-í-térék-èr-à   òvá-éndà p-òngàndà
      SM1-OM2-OM9-cook-APPL-FV 2-guests 16-9.house
      's/he cooks it for them at the house.' (Herero, Kempson et al. 2013: 78)

Example (161) shows a verb form with two full overt noun phrases. Example (162) shows the omission of the class 2 noun òváéndà 'guests' which is instead indicated through the class 2 object marker vé. A similar strategy is employed in (163) which shows the use of the class 9 object marker í- to refer to the class 9 nominal ònyàmà 'meat'. However, example (164) shows that it is not possible to include object markers for both the object òváéndà 'guests' and ònyàmà 'meat'.

Kempson et al. (2013) suggest that the constraint on multiple unfixed nodes may play a role in object marking restrictions in Herero. Object markers across Bantu are assumed to be projected onto a locally unfixed node. Whether the object marker refers to a direct or an indirect object argument does not affect the details of the account (Marten et al. 2008; Kempson et al. 2013). However, employing an unfixed node as part of the processing strategies captures the prohibition on the presence of more than one object marker. This would result in two unfixed nodes of the same modality at the same time and represent a contravention of the Unique Unfixed Node Constraint. In basic terms, if object markers project locally unfixed nodes, then two object markers cannot occur since two locally unfixed nodes cannot co-occur.

Thus, from a DS perspective, the restrictions on object marking in Bantu languages result naturally from the tree logic. However, one question remains. In many Bantu languages one object can occur in a given verb form (as is seen in Rangi, Swahili, siSwati and Herero amongst others). However, in a number of other languages multiple object markers can co-occur (in Tswana, Rundi and Kinyarwanda for example). If the restriction on the co-occurrence of multiple object markers is a corollary of the tree logic which is assumed to apply universally, then it is difficult to account for this cross-linguistic variation.

An appropriate account of those Bantu languages in which multiple object markers are permitted might be one under which these markers are projected onto a complex that is dominated by a single underspecified tree node address. This means that whilst multiple object markers can be projected onto different nodes, these nodes are dominated by only a single unfixed tree relation. An approach similar to this was taken to parsing multiple nominal phrases with underspecified tree node addresses in languages that exhibit scrambling (Kiaer 2007; Marten et al. 2008). This analysis demonstrates how each node that is induced by an object marker is fixed immediately upon introduction and, crucially, before the next object marker is parsed (see also McCormack 2008 for discussion of a pragmatic notion of constructive case). Such accounts therefore necessarily also employ the concept of underspecification – although the underspecification remains restricted to a single overarching unfixed tree node.

The difference between languages in which multiple object markers are allowed and those in which they are not, would therefore be seen as the result of language-specific differences. In some languages, the lexical actions encoded by the object markers would enable the construction of a 'complex' dominated by a single underspecified tree node address, while in other languages this would not be possible. Such language-specific differences can also be seen to mirror micro-variation in languages from other languages families, such as the range of variants of the Person Case Constraint.

7.1.4. *Word order variation in Japanese and Korean*

One of the challenges which emerges in relation to head-final languages is how speakers and hearers resolve the apparent tension between linear word order and head-finality. The expectation may be that verb-final languages such as Japanese and Korean would pose a challenge to the DS approach due to emphasis the framework places on the left-to-right nature of the parsing/production process. In the accounts presented in this study so far, the verb has been the major projector of structure. Information that has been provided by nominal arguments has been projected onto unfixed nodes, with the fixing of these tree node addresses becoming possible only after the verb is parsed. However, in verb-final languages, the main projector of structure – the verb – is not encountered until all of the other elements have already been processed. As will be shown, this does not pose a problem for the Dynamic Syntax approach which instead assumes the structure can be built before the verb is encountered in these languages.

It was initially assumed that in verb-final languages such as Japanese, no projection of structure was possible until the verb was parsed (Pritchett 1992). However, it is now thought that this is not the case. Moreover, there is experimental evidence that supports the idea that, despite the final placement of the verb, speakers of verb-final languages such as Japanese carry out the building of structure incrementally and do not 'wait' until the verb is encountered to establish the intended meaning (Inoue & Fodor 1995; Kamide & Mitchell 1999; Miyamoto 2002; Ferreira & Yoshita 2003; Aoshima et al. 2004). This observation can be naturally captured using the DS approach, which hinges on the concepts of underspecificaiton and the progressive enrichment of forms (Kempson & Kiaer 2009). The application of this in Japanese and Korean will be explored through a discussion of DS accounts of word order variability in these languages.

In Japanese, a verb can exist independently of an overt subject. This means that an utterance such as *tobu-da* which is comprised of the verb *tobu* 'fly' and the past tense marker *-da* can convey a meaning along the lines of 'some individual flew' (Seraku 2013a). One of the first issues to address is therefore the radical pro-drop nature of Japanese. To reflect the pro-drop nature of the language (which also includes omission of object arguments), it is assumed that the verb provides considerably more than an annotation of the logical predicate. Rather, the verb is assumed to trigger a complex of actions that induces the building of the skeletal predicate-argument structure, including the introduction of the argument nodes in addition to the predicate node itself. These argument slots are annotated with metavariables that license contextual identification. For example, the verb *tobu-* 'fly' can be considered to project an open proposition with a metavariable for the situation term and a metavariable for the subject term. The metavariables, as is standard, are accompanied by the requirement to receive update to a full formula value – indicated by $?\exists x.Fo(x)$. The tree structure below is from Seraku (2013a) and includes the decoration of the subject node with the metavariable $\mathbf{V}$. If the value for this node is contextually accessible, then $\mathbf{V}$ can be saturated by the pragmatic action SUBSTITUTION and be updated to a full value such as Fo(bird').

(165)   Parsing: *tobu* 'fly'

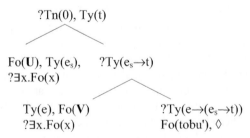

Before the verb is accessed however, a number of argument phrases may also have been parsed. The proposal is that in verb-final languages, structure building occurs in an incremental left-to-right manner (in much the same way as in verb-initial languages) and that the establishment of propositional structure is licensed even before the verb is parsed.

Japanese exhibits a relatively free order of constituents before the verb. This flexibility in word order does not present a challenge for the DS approach, since the system does not rely on positioning to encode syntactic roles (see Chapter 4). Rather, these nominal expressions are considered to be projected onto unfixed nodes and the case markers subsequently play a central role in establishing the function of the nominals in the emergent tree, as well as in fixing the eventual tree node addresses of these elements. Consider examples (166) and (167), which show that *Porco* (a name) and *ringo* 'apple' can appear in either order before the verb form but are marked with the same case marking in each instance.

(166) Porco-ga   ring-o   tabe-ta
       Porco-NOM apple-ACC   eat-PAST
       'Porco ate an apple' (Japanese, Seraku 2013a: 19)

(167) Ringo-o   Porco-ga   tabe-ta
       apple-ACC Porco-NOM eat-PAST
       'Porco ate an apple' (Japanese, Seraku 2013a: 19)

Assuming that noun phrases in Japanese are projected onto unfixed nodes, parsing an unmarked form of *Porco* would mean that the noun could ultimately end up as the subject, direct or indirect object of the clause since it would simply decorate a structure the relative position of which is identified in only very general terms as $\langle \uparrow * \rangle \text{Tn}(0)$ – i.e. the current node is dominated by the root node. However, since in these examples *Porco* hosts the nominative marker -*ga*, its eventual position in the tree is restricted to that of the immediate daughter of a type *t*-requiring node (indicated by $\langle \uparrow_0 \rangle \text{Ty}(t)$) which means that the node can receive a fixed tree address as the subject node. Similarly, the accusative case marker -*o* introduces a requirement that the node is the immediate daughter of a predicate-requiring node $?\langle \uparrow_0 \rangle \text{Ty}$ (e→t), meaning that this nominal can also receive a fixed tree node address.

Overall therefore, each noun phrase is presumed to be projected with a weakly specified tree relation. However, this relation can be enriched to the particular argument node which the noun will assume within the emergent structure as a result of parsing the case marker. The variation in word order therefore makes no difference to the final tree and both examples can be parsed by recourse to the same steps. Case can therefore be seen to be central to the DS account of the establishment of propositional structure in Japanese, and can be seen to interact intimately with the process of structural growth and to constrain updates of the underspecified structure projected by NPs.[39]

A similar situation can be seen in Korean where, again, two case-marked nominals can appear before the verbal complex, with either order possible, as in examples (168) and (169) below.

(168) Jina-ka   sakwa-rul mek-ess-ta
       Jina-NOM apple-ACC eat-PAST-DECL
       'Jina ate an apple'   (Korean, Kempson et al. 2009: 143)

(169) Sakwa-rul Jina-ka   mek-ess-ta
       apple-ACC Jina-NOM eat-PAST-DECL
       'Jina ate an apple'   (Korean, Kempson et al. 2009: 143)

For Korean, it is also proposed that argument nodes can be introduced into the emerging tree independently of the projection of the predicate itself. This allows for the incremental projection of structure from the words encountered (in this case nouns) even before the verb is parsed (Kiaer & Kempson 2005). A corollary of this is that as long as the nominals are case-marked, the structure building process involved for parsing example (168) and example (169) proceeds in exactly the same manner regardless of the position of the nouns, as was seen above for Japanese.

Japanese and Korean also exhibit 'long-distance scrambling' in which the relative free order of nouns can also be seen across clausal boundaries. This can be seen in the examples below.[40]

(170) Sakwa-rul Mina-ka   Jina-ka   mekessta-ko malhayssta
       apple-ACC Mina-NOM Jina-NOM ate-COMP   said
       'Jina said that Mina ate an apple'   (Korean, Kempson et al. 2009: 143)

(171) syorui-o   keisatu-ga zyaanarisuto-ga yonda   to
       the document-ACC police-NOM journalist-NOM   handed   COMP
       koohyoo-sita
       reported
       'The document, the police reported that the journalist had read'
                                              (Japanese, Kempson & Kiaer 2010: 28)

---

[39] This contrasts with the system in Bantu languages where there is no overt marking of case and as such, strategies related to morphological case are not available for the update of underspecified tree node relations.

[40] The focus will be on modelling the flow of information in long-distance scrambling constructions in Korean. However, in many instances, similar assumptions as those made for Korean can be made for Japanese since it is also head-final and involves similar use of case and prosodic cues. The interested reader is referred to (Kempson & Kiaer 2009; Seraku 2013a) for more on the specifics of the construal associated with similar parses in Japanese.

On the basis that nominals are projected onto unfixed nodes, the challenge posed by examples such as (170) and (171) is that these structures might be expected to involve the presence of more than one unfixed node at a given time, in direct contravention of the Unique Unfixed Node Constraint. Whilst one nominal in each example hosts a distinct case marker, the following two noun phrases do not host distinct case markers and appear in immediate succession. Despite the existence of more than one expression at a distance from the verb with which these argument nodes need to unify, Kempson & Kiaer (2010) propose that such constructions do not contradict the constraint on the co-occurrence of multiple unfixed nodes.

Recall that DS makes available three discrete processes for introducing structurally underspecified relations into the tree: LOCAL *ADJUNCTION, *ADJUNC-TION and GENERALISED *ADJUNCTION. As Kempson & Kiaer (2009b) observe, there is nothing to prohibit one of these processes from feeding into another. In other words, an unfixed node can feed into a locally unfixed node, and vice versa. Such a process would involve the construction of an unfixed type-t-requiring node at the left periphery, from which successive steps of LOCAL *ADJUNCTION can apply, inducing partial propositional structure containing locally unfixed nodes which can receive update from the case information that appears on the nouns.

The examples involving long-distance scrambling can therefore be captured by recourse to the standard DS machinery. The stages involved are as follows. The rule of *ADJUNCTION introduces an unfixed type-t-requiring node. The first two nouns in the left-peripheral sequence are both assumed to be, in turn, associated with the building and decorating of a node constructed from this node by LOCAL *ADJUNCTION. The case marking on the first nominal fixes the relation of the newly built locally unfixed node to its locally dominating node. For the second NP however, the case specification is considered to act as a filter on output (rather than fixing tree node addresses) and enables the pointer to return from the second type-e node to the top node, leaving this node unfixed both in relation to its intermediate dominating node and to the higher dominating node.

Subsequently, the standard stages of introducing a matrix subject node occur: a locally unfixed node is introduced and the subject relation is subsequently fixed as a result of parsing the nominative marker -*ga*. The rule of GENERALISED ADJUNCTION then introduces a generally unfixed node and one further process of introducing a subject relation in order to parse the second *ga*-marked nominal. Once this occurs, the weak relation between the type-t-requiring node and the root node is enriched. The verb can subsequently be parsed and the predicate-argument structure can be fleshed out following the standard assumptions made for tree growth in the language more broadly as the unfixed nodes (hosting the two arguments) receive fixed tree node addresses. This process is argued to simply involve the interaction between general processes of tree growth and is considered to be applicable for both Korean and Japanese.

As Kempson & Kiaer (2009) note, the local nature of the construal of the constituents in the clause is predicted in a straightforward manner from the core assumptions of the DS approach. The processing of the two nominals in a multiple long-distance dependency relation involves just one initial step of *ADJUNCTION and then subsequent successive applications of LOCAL *ADJUNCTION. In all but the final instance, there is pointer movement back to the intermediate ?Ty(t) node once the unfixed node has received its type-assignment and the tree node address has been fully specified upon parsing the case marker. This is reminiscent also of the discussion on Japanese clefts in which all but the final nominal must be case-marked in order to ensure the resolution of the unfixed tree node addresses of the nouns (cleft constructions and multiple foci in Japanese in Section 7.1.2).

The broad picture is therefore that in languages which work in this way, upon encountering a case-marked NP, there are two choices available: either the NP can immediately be fixed within its local domain as a result of the case marking, or the tree node address can remain underspecified until a relatively 'late' stage in the process as long as it is resolved before the end of the parse.[41] In this way, when the parser encounters a string of two nouns which carry the same case marker, these nouns are assumed to be associated with two discrete structures at two different levels of embedding. In example (170), the first nominative-marked NP is considered to have induced a step of LOCAL *ADJUNCTION and be immediately identified as the subject of the matrix clause. However, in order to parse the second nominative-marked phrase, the only remaining option is for the rule of GENERALISED *ADJUNCTION to apply, thereby inducing a subordination relation. An indefinitely embedded structure is subsequently induced and in order for the parse to proceed, a fixed tree relation has to be established.

Experimental evidence supports the idea that Korean parsers can incorporate case information directly into the structure building process, without having to wait until the very end of the parse when the verb is encountered (Kim 1999). This is similar to the proposal that is made for Japanese. Miyamoto (2002) claims that a number of strategies converge to enable the step-by-step buildup of structure in Japanese and the possibility of establishing propositional structure, even before the verb is encountered. These include: (i) the construction of underspecified tree relations; (ii) the constructive use of case to induce fixed structural relations within the tree; and (iii) and the indication by case markers of higher phrasal boundaries (analogous to the prosodic cues in Korean).

Underspecification and update can be seen to be central to the approach developed here. The flexibly-ordered sequence of nouns is only acceptable since they can induce partial structure which is built via the application of the *ADJUNCTION rules. However, the way in which these rules can interact – and feed into each other, is tightly regulated by the Unique Unified Node Constraint. In this way, word order effects in Japanese and Korean can be seen to be regulated by the same mechanism that was considered responsible for the other patterning

---

[41] Recall that multiple parsing/production strategies may be available for any given string in the DS approach so this does not represent a radical assumption.

restrictions discussed in the present section, as well as auxiliary placement alternation in Rangi.

The proposal is that the DS approach is also able to characterise the relatively flexible word order (and pro-drop) nature of head-final languages such as Korean and Japanese in a relatively straightforward way. This can be done without recourse to any mechanisms which have not already been introduced in the DS approach and the current discussion which has focused primarily on head-initial languages. Verbs build full propositional structure which is associated with (semantically) underspecified arguments. These arguments are projected in the same way as they would be if they were projected from anaphoric expressions. In contrast to the analysis presented for Bantu languages and Romance and Greek, nouns in Japanese and Korean are considered to be responsible not just for the decoration of a single node but for the projection of a structural template. The verb also provides annotation for the predicate node, as well as introducing a skeletal predicate-argument structure which includes the construction of nodes for each of the arguments in addition to the structure for the predicate itself. However, these argument nodes are annotated with metavariables. When the verb is parsed, it projects a full propositional template relating to the predicate node and the array of argument nodes with which it is associated. If any of the argument nodes of this template have already been introduced, this newly introduced structure will simply collapse with the nodes already present in the tree since two nodes with the same tree node address will be one and the same node. This collapse is entirely harmless, and has previously been seen to be central to the account provided for auxiliary constructions in Bantu (for modelling both multiple occurrences of subject markers, as well as for modelling the flow of information between the auxiliary form and the main verb).

7.2. SUMMARY

The chapter has presented an overview of the Unique Unfixed Node Constraint and a number of manifestations of this constraint across a selection of unrelated languages. It has shown the accounts which have been formulated in DS terms of clitic placement in Spanish and varieties of Modern Greek, multiple foci in Japanese clefts, multiple object marking in Bantu languages and word order variation in Japanese and Korean. All of the aforementioned phenomena have been, at least in part, attributed to the effects of the restriction on the co-occurrence of multiple unfixed nodes. The discussion presented in the current chapter emphasises the strength of the framework in drawing out cross-linguistic parallels, at least in terms of processing. Since distinct phenomena in unrelated languages can be seen to employ similar processing strategies and be affected by similar restrictions.

Viewed from this perspective, the DS approach therefore presents a strong claim: what may appear to be language-specific morphosyntactic phenomena, can instead be explained by reference to the dynamics of the process of incremental update which takes place in the same way across languages. Indeed, this is the approach taken to syntax more widely. The intricacies of morphosyntactic variation are instead seen to be the result of frozen reflexes of more general processes of incremental structure building. Whilst here this approach has been used to account for variation in unrelated languages, similar routes could also be used to capture variation on a micro-level, including subtle differences between closely related languages and/or varieties and dialects.

8

CONCLUSION

8.1. SUMMARY

The goal of Dynamic Syntax is to model the dynamics of natural language and the establishment of propositional structure involved in the real-time parsing/production process. The step-by-step build-up of information during the interpretation process is represented through the incremental growth of binary semantic trees. Tree growth involves the unfolding of one partial tree into another in which the relations holding within the tree are progressively specified and the values that annotate the tree node are enriched. At the outset of the book, it was claimed that Dynamic Syntax represents a radical departure from more traditional models of syntactic theory. One of the ways in which DS differs from other approaches is through the attempt to model the real-time online nature of the parsing/production process and the way in which semantic representations give rise to meaning. The goal of this study has been to develop an approach to Bantu clause structure which relies on precisely these dynamics and which revolves around the incremental nature of this process. To this end, the present study has explored a range of issues involved in the establishment of meaning in Bantu languages, drawing primarily on the East African Bantu languages Rangi and Swahili.

Chapter 2 presented an introduction to the Dynamic Syntax framework. It outlined the driving force behind the approach – the aim to provide a model of the cognitive architecture which underlies natural language parsing and production. The chapter presented an overview of the formal architecture used to express and define these processes and the ways in which tree growth can occur – through cross-linguistically available transition rules, language-specific lexical input and contextual pragmatic enrichment. This chapter provided the theoretical foundation necessary to understand and engage with the account provided throughout the rest of the study.

An in-depth discussion of the issues involved in the Dynamic Syntax approach to modelling Bantu clause structure was the focus of Chapter 3. The chapter centred around the mechanisms used to process each of the core elements of the clause: the contribution made by the subject expression (when present), subject and object agreement, as well as the verb stem and any verbal extensions were explored. The chapter built on existing work examining Bantu languages and presented a unified, up-to-date unified account of the properties of the Bantu clause.

Underspecification and update are key principles in the DS approach. Underspecication is considered to be the property which allows for the manipulation of information throughout the tree building process. Chapter 4 explored the role of underspecification in a selection of domains which lie at the heart of contemporary investigations into Bantu morphosyntax. It looked at the underspecified nature of the Bantu verb and the associated underspecification in terms of temporal distinctions. It also presented an overview of the way in which underspecification and update have been employed in previous DS accounts of both inversion constructions and passive constructions in the Bantu languages.

Chapter 5 took steps towards developing an account of some of the key strategies that are used to encode negation across the Bantu family, from the perspective of the Dynamic Syntax framework. It presented key questions that arise in relation to a DS account of negation in Bantu, whilst also engaging with the central questions that such construction types raise. It developed an account of sentential negation in main clauses in Swahili and Rangi, as well as exploring the issues involved in accounts of negation in non-main clause contexts in these languages.

Chapter 6 presented an analysis of the typologically and comparatively unusual word order alternation found in Rangi. The alternation between pre-verbal and post-verbal auxiliary placement poses a challenge for a static theory of syntax, both in terms of the temporal interpretation of the clause and the syntactic constraints under which it operates. However, under the DS approach, this word order alternation can be seen to result from the independent constraint operative in the framework which curtails underspecification. Not only is the DS approach therefore able to account for the patterning phenomena exhibited by this language, it can actually be seen to predict possible and prohibited orders.

The predictive power of the Dynamic Syntax framework was also observed in Chapter 7 which examined the parallels between accounts that have been developed for a wide range of phenomena across unrelated languages. The chapter centred on an exploration of the formal constraint operative in the DS system which has been termed the Unique Unfixed Node Constraint. The manifestations of this phenomenon in varieties of Greek, Spanish, Japanese and Korean were examined alongside a discussion of other possible reflexes of this restriction within the Bantu languages.

8.2. Concluding remarks

A number of key concepts have emerged over the course of this study. The nature of the DS approach and the way in which it seeks to capture the real-time parsing/production process, means that the establishment of propositional structure is always seen to involve underspecified values which must as a matter of course receive attendant update. The introduction of a metavariable and the subsequent update of this placeholder to a fully-specified formula value was shown to occur across a number of distinct phenomena, including with auxiliary forms which build fixed structure, as well as with subject markers which restrict the possible referents with which a subject can be identified. Similarly, the way in which unfixed tree nodes receive fully-specified tree node addresses and copula forms can be enriched from other values, also reflects underspecification.

Another feature of the DS formalism which has been employed throughout the course of the analysis is the re-building of structure. Whilst the re-building of structure is provided by the DS architecture and has previously been seen in other accounts developed from this perspective, the centrality of this is brought to the fore in the current discussion, particularly as it pertains to auxiliary constructions. Crucially, in these contexts, the rebuilding of structure is reflected in the interaction between pre-stem tense-aspect markers and verb stems, the distribution of subject marking, as well as auxiliary and verb forms in compound constructions. This feature was seen to be central to the ability to develop a monoclausal analysis of compound verbal constructions in which compound constructions are associated with a single event. This was considered to reflect the observation that auxiliary constructions enable a wider range of tense-aspect combinations to be encoded for a single event whilst being associated with complex structure.

The third key theme that emerged over the course of the discussion was the context-dependent nature of interpretation from the dynamic perspective. This was seen for example, in relation to the homophony that was observed in the modelling of Bantu morphology. Whilst homophony may represent a challenge to some approaches, the context-dependent nature of the DS approach means that this can often be naturally captured through reference to lexical entries which contain a set of complex triggering conditions – i.e. triggering conditions which reflect the different lexical actions that will apply given the specifics of the context in which the item is parsed. In this way, DS is ideally suited for capturing the context-dependent nature of the parsing/production process, whilst Bantu languages lend themselves to an incremental approach due to the nature of their morphology and the close relationship between morphology and syntax. The framework was shown to be able to capture both the behaviour of Swahili and the intricacies of the Rangi data through, in most instances, employing the pre-existing tools of the theoretical approach.

The Dynamic Syntax approach seeks to develop a grammar formalism which reflects the online manner in which natural language is parsed and produced. In the pursuit of this goal, the tools and mechanisms which have been previously assumed to be available, can be seen to naturally capture a range of morphosyntactic phenomena, drawing on a combination of lexical input, computational rules and pragmatic update for the incremental establishment of propositional structure. However, the framework can also be extended to a variety of other linguistic questions in a straightforward manner. Recent years have seen discussion of the application of the tools of Dynamic Syntax to modelling interaction and dialogue. This arises from the observation that binary semantic trees need not be constructed only by a single speaker/hearer but can in fact be constructed between two interlocutors. A model of interaction therefore follows in a straightforward manner and dialogue can be seen as an immediate consequence of the grammar formalism, without need for an intermediate level of representation. Discourse can therefore be captured by recourse to 'shared' trees, with speakers and hearers involved in the cooperative act of communication.

Other possible avenues for future investigation that arise as a result of the current discussion relate to a more fully-specified account of negation. Whilst the contribution made in morphological terms are captured in the current work, the details of how best to represent negation from a DS perspective in formal terms, remain to be further developed. Similarly, the discussion drew out parallels between different construction types and the ability to capture these through recourse to the standard tools made available in the framework. Under the standard assumptions, cross-linguistic variation can be assumed to be the result of the lexicon. However, the precise origins of cross-linguistic variation, particularly on the micro-level remains to be examined in further detail, alongside a discussion of how this relates to processes of language change.

One of the observations that emerged is also that the tree building process in unrelated languages can be captured through recourse to similar processing strategies, drawing out cross-linguistic parallels in terms of universally applicable constraints on the establishment of propositional structure. As the empirical coverage of the framework extends, new parallels may also emerge. However, one of the strengths of the framework remains its ability to capture a wide range of phenomena, without the need to postulate independent rules or constraints which are not embedded in higher cognitive processes.

REFERENCES

AOSHIMA, SACHIKO, COLIN PHILLIPS, & AMY WEINBERG, 2004. 'Processing filler-gap dependencies in a head-final language', *Journal of Memory and Language* 51(1). 23–54.

ASHTON, ETHEL O. 1944. *Swahili grammar*. London: Longman.

BEARTH, THOMAS, 2003. 'Syntax', in Derek Nurse & Gérard Philippson (eds.), *The Bantu languages*, London: Routledge. 121–142.

BLACKBURN, PATRICK, & WILFRED MEYER-VIOL. 1994. 'Linguistics, logic and finite trees', *Bulletin of Interest Group of Pure and Applied Logic* 2(1). 2–39.

BOTNE, ROBERT, 1989. 'Reconstruction of a grammaticalized auxiliary in Bantu', *Studies in the Linguistic Sciences* 19(2). 169–186.

BOUZOUITA, MIRIAM, 2002. *Clitic placement in Old and Modern Spanish: A dynamic account*. London: Kings College London MSc dissertation.

BOUZOUITA, MIRIAM, 2007. 'Processing factors in syntactic variation and change: Clitics in Medieval and Renaissance Spanish' in Miriam Butt & Tracy Holloway King (eds.), *17th International Conference on Historical Linguistics, Madison, WI*. Amsterdam: John Benjamins. Series 4, Current issues in linguistic theory. 51–71.

BOUZOUITA, MIRIAM, 2008a. 'At the syntax-pragmatics interface: Clitics in the history of Spanish', in Robin Cooper & Ruth Kempson (eds.), *Language evolution and change*. London: College Publications. 223–285.

BOUZOUITA, MIRIAM, 2008b. *The diachronic development of Spanish clitic placement*. London: Kings College London Ph.D. dissertation.

BOUZOUITA, MIRIAM, & STERGIOS CHATZIKYRIAKIDIS, 2009. 'Clitics as calcified processing strategies, in Miriam Butt & Tracy Holloway King (eds.), *17th International Conference on Historical Linguistics, Madison, WI*. Stanford, CA: CSLI Publications. 188–207.

BRESNAN, JOAN, & SAM A. MCHOMBO, 1987. 'Topic, pronoun, and agreement in Chichewa', *Language* 63(4). 741–782.

BRESNAN, JOAN, & LIOBA MOSHI, 1990. 'Object asymmetries in comparative Bantu syntax', *Linguistic Inquiry* 21(2). 147–185.

CAMMENGA, JELLE, 2004. *Igikuria phonology and morphology: A Bantu language of South-West Kenya and North-West Tanzania*. Cologne: Rüdiger Köppe Verlag.

CANN, RONNIE, 2006. 'Semantic underspecification and the interpretation of copular clauses in English', in Klaus von Heusinger & Ken Turner (eds.), *Where semantics meets pragmatics*. Oxford: Elsevier. 307–335.

CANN, RONNIE, 2007. 'Towards a dynamic account of be in English', in Ileana Comorowski & Klaus von Heusinger (eds.), *Existence: Syntax and semantics*. Dordrecht: Kluwer Academic Publishers. 13–48.

CANN, RONNIE, 2011. 'Towards an account of the English auxiliary system: Building interpretations incrementally', in Ruth Kempson, Eleni Gregoromichelaki & Christine Howes (eds.), *The dynamics of lexical interfaces*. Stanford, CA: CSLI publications. 279–317.

CANN, RONNIE, & RUTH KEMPSON, 2008. 'Production pressures, syntactic change and the emergence of clitic pronouns', in Robin Cooper & Ruth Kempson (eds.), *Language in flux: Dialogue coordination, language variation, change and evolution*. London: College Publications. 221–263.

CANN, RONNIE, RUTH KEMPSON, LUTZ MARTEN, & MASAYUKI OTSUKA, 2005a. 'Right node raising, coordination and the dynamics of language processing', *Lingua* 115(4). 503–525.

CANN, RONNIE, LUTZ MARTEN, & RUTH KEMPSON, 2005b. *The Dynamics of Language*. Oxford: Elsevier.

CARSTON, ROBYN. 1996. 'Enrichment and loosening: Complementary processes in deriving the proposition expressed', *UCL Working Papers in Linguistics* 8 (1996). 61–88.

CHATZIKYRIAKIDIS, STERGIOS, 2009. 'The person case constraint in Modern Greek: A unified dynamic syntax account', *Newcastle Working Papers in Linguistics* 15(2009). 40–62.

CHATZIKYRIAKIDIS, STERGIOS, 2010. *Clitics in four dialects of Modern Greek: A dynamic account*. Ph.D. dissertation. Kings College London.

CHATZIKYRIAKIDIS, STERGIOS, & HANNAH GIBSON, 2017. 'The Bantu-Romance-Greek connection revisited: Processing constraints in auxiliary and clitic placement from a cross-linguistic perspective', *Glossa* 2(1). 1–39.

CHAVULA, JEAN JOSEPHINE, 2016. *Verbal derivation and valency in Citumbuka*. Ph.D. dissertation. University of Leiden.

CHO, SUNGDAI, JOHN WHITMAN, & YUKO YANAGIDA, 2008. 'Clefts in Japanese and Korean', *Proceedings from the Annual Meeting of the Chicago Linguistics Society* 44(1). 61–77.

DEMUTH, KATHERINE, & MARK JOHNSON. 1989. 'Interactions between discourse functions and agreement in Setswana', *Journal of African Languages and Linguistics* 11(1989). 22–35.

DEVOS, MAUD, MICHAEL KASOMBO TSHIBANDA, & JOHAN VAN DER AUWERA, 2010. 'Jespersen cycles in Kanincin: double, triple and maybe even quadruple negation', *Africana Linguistica* 16(2010). 155–182.

DEVOS, MAUD, & JOHAN VAN DER AUWERA, 2013. 'Jespersen cycles in Bantu: double and triple negation', *Journal of African Languages and Linguistics* 34(2). 205–274.

DUNHAM, MARGARET. 1996–2004. Corpus langi. http://lacito.vjf.cnrs.fr/ALC/La nguages/Langi_popup.htm (10 November 2016).

DUNHAM, MARGARET, 2005. *Eléments de description du langi, langue Bantu F.33 de Tanzanie*. Collection Langues et littératures de l'Afrique noire SELAF 413. Louvain-Paris-Dudley MA: Peeters.

FERREIRA, VICTOR, & HIROMI YOSHITA, 2003. 'Given-new ordering effects on the production of scrambled sentences in Japanese', *Journal of Psycholinguistic Research* 32(2003). 573–596.

GIBSON, HANNAH, 2012. *Auxiliary placement in Rangi: A dynamic syntax perspective*. Ph.D. dissertation. SOAS, University of London.

GIBSON, HANNAH, 2016. 'A unified dynamic account of auxiliary placement in Rangi', *Lingua* 184. 79–103.

GIBSON, HANNAH, & LUTZ MARTEN, 2016. 'Variation and grammaticalisation in Bantu complex verbal constructions: The dynamics of information growth in Swahili, Rangi and siSwati', in Lea Nash & Pollet Samvelian (eds.), Approaches to complex predicates. Leiden: Brill, 70–109.

GIBSON, HANNAH, & VERA WILHELMSEN, 2015. 'Cycles of negation in Rangi and Mbugwe', *African Linguistica* 21(2015). 233–257.

GREGOROMICHELAKI, ELENI, 2006. *Conditionals in dynamic syntax*. Ph.D. dissertation. King's College London.

GÜLDEMANN, TOM. 1996. *Verbalmorphologie under nebenprädikationen im Bantu*. Bochum: Brockmeyer.

GÜLDEMANN, TOM. 1999. 'The genesis of verbal negation in Bantu and its dependency on functional features and clause types', in Jean-Marie Hombert and Larry M. Hyman (eds.), *Bantu historical linguistics: Theoretical and empirical linguistics*. Stanford, CA: CSLI. 545–587.

HEINE, BERND, ULRIKE CLAUDI, & FRIEDERIKE HÜNNEMEYER. 1991. *Grammaticalization: A conceptual framework*. Chicago, IL: University of Chicago Press.

HEINE, BERND, & MECHTHILD REH. 1984. *Grammaticalization and reanalysis in African Languages*. Hamburg: Helmut Buske.

HIRAIWA, KEN, & SHINICHIRO ISHIHARA, 2011. 'Syntactic metamorphosis', *Syntax* 15(2). 142–180.

HORNSTEIN, NORBERT. 1990. *As time goes by: Tense and universal grammar*. Cambridge, MA: MIT Press.

INOUE, ATSU, & JANET DEAN FODOR. 1995. 'Information-paced parsing of Japanese', in Reiko Mazuka & Noriko Nagai (eds.), Japanese Syntactic Processing. Hillsdale, NJ: Lawrence Erlbaum. 9–64.

JERRO, KYLE, 2016. *The syntax and semantics of applicative morphology in Bantu*. Ph.D. dissertation. University of Texas at Austin.

KAMBA MUZENGA, JEAN-GEORGES 1981. *Les formes verbales négatives dans les langues bantoues*. Tervuren: Musée Royal de l'Afrique Centrale.

KAMIDE, YUKI, & DON G. MITCHELL, 1999. 'Incremental pre-head attachment in Japanese parsing', *Language and Cognitive Processes* 14(5/6). 631–662.

KAMP, HANS & UWE REYLE, 1993. *From Discourse to Logic: an introduction to modeltheoretic semantics, formal logic and Discourse Representation Theory*. Hingham, MA: Kluwer.

KEMPSON, RUTH, n.d. *Japanese scrambling as growth of semantic representation*. Ms. King's College London.

KEMPSON, RUTH, RONNIE CANN, & LUTZ MARTEN, 2008. 'Treegrowth dynamics', in Cristiano Chesi (ed.), *Directions in derivations*. London: Emerald. 49–82.

KEMPSON, RUTH, RONNIE CANN, & LUTZ MARTEN, 2013. 'Tree growth dynamics', *Studies in Linguistics* 6(2013). 49–81.

KEMPSON, RUTH, & STERGIOS CHATZIKYRIAKIDIS, 2009. 'The person case constraint as a treegrowth property', Ms., Kings College London.

KEMPSON, RUTH, ELENI GREGOROMICHELAKI, & CHRISTINE HOWES (eds.), 2010. *The dynamics of lexical interfaces*. Stanford, CA: CSLI Publications.

KEMPSON, RUTH, ELENI GREGOROMICHELAKI, MATTHEW PURVER, WILFRIED MEYER-VIOL, CHRISTINE HOWES, PATRICK HEALEY, ARASH ESHGHI, JULIAN HOUGH, GRAHAM WHITE, & RONNIE CANN, 2011. 'On the processing of elipsis: A preliminary report'. Unpublished ms.

KEMPSON, RUTH, & JIEUN KIAER, 2009. 'Japanese scrambling: The dynamics of on-line Processing', in Hiroto Hoshi (ed.), *The dynamics and mechanism of language: Perspectives from linguistics and cognitive neuroscience*. Tokyo: Kuroshio Press: 5–45.

KEMPSON, RUTH, & JIEUN KIAER, 2010. 'Multiple long-distance scrambling: Syntax as reflections of processing', *Journal of Linguistics* 46(1). 127–192.

KEMPSON, RUTH, JIEUN KIAER, & RONNIE, CANN, 2008. 'Topic and focus at the peripheries: the dynamics of tree growth', in Benjamin Shaer, Philippa Cook, Werner Frey & Claudia Maienborn (eds.), *Dislocated elements in discourse: Syntactic, semantic and discourse perspectives*, New York: Routledge, 141–170.

KEMPSON, RUTH, JIEUN KIAER, & RONNIE CANN, 2009. 'Periphery effects and the dynamics of tree growth', in Benjamin Shaer, Philippa Cook, Werner Frey & Claudia Maienborn (eds.), *Dislocated elements in discourse: Syntactic semantics and pragmatic perspectives*, New York: Routledge, 141–172.

KEMPSON, RUTH, & LUTZ MARTEN, 2002. 'Pronouns, agreement, and the dynamic construction of verb phrase interpretation: A Dynamic Syntax approach to Bantu clause structure', *Linguistic Analysis* 32(3–4). 471–504.

KEMPSON, RUTH, LUTZ MARTEN, & NHLANHLA THWALA, 2011b. 'SiSwati clefts: The meeting ground of context and contrast', in Ruth Kempson, Eleni Gregoromichelaki and Christine Howes (eds.), *The dynamics of lexical interfaces*. Stanford, CA: CSLI Publications. 23–60.

KEMPSON, RUTH, WILFRIED MEYER-VIOL, & DOV GABBAY, 2001. *Dynamic syntax: The flow of language understanding*. London: Blackwell Publishing.

KEMPSON, RUTH, & LIU WEI, 2017. 'Chinese cleft structures and the dynamics of Processing', *Transactions of the Philological Society* 116(1). 91–117.

KIAER, JIEUN, 2007. *Processing and Interfaces in Syntactic Theory: The case of Korean*. Ph.D. dissertation. Kings College London.

KIAER, JIEUN, & RUTH KEMPSON, 2005. 'Pro-active parsing of Korean scrambling' in John Alderete, Chung-hye Han & Alexei Kochetov (eds.), *24th West Coast Conference on Formal Linguistics*. Somerville, MA: Cascadilla Proceedings Project. 209–217.

KIM, YONGJIN. 1999. 'The effects of case marking information on Korean sentence Processing', *Language and Cognitive Processes* 14(5–6). 687–714.

KLEIN, WOLFGANG. 1994. *Time in Language*. London: Routledge.

KURODA, SHIGEYUKI, 2005. *Nihongo kara Mita Seisei Bunpo* [Generative grammar from the perspective of Japanese]. Tokyo: Iwanami.

LUCAS, CHRISTOPHER, '2014. Indefinites and negative concord in Maltese: Towards a dynamic account', in Albert Borg, Sandro Caruana and Alexandra Vella (eds.), *Perspectives on Maltese linguistics*. Berlin: Akademie Verlag. 225–248.

MARLO, MICHAEL, 2015. 'On the number of object markers in Bantu languages', *Journal of African Languages and Linguistics* 36(1). 1–65.

MARTEN, LUTZ, 2002. *At the syntax-pragmatics interface: Verbal underspecification and concept formation in dynamic syntax.* Oxford: Oxford University Press.

MARTEN, LUTZ, 2003. 'The dynamics of Bantu applied verbs: An analysis at the syntax-pragmatics interface', in Kézié K. Lébikaza (ed.), *Actes due 3e Congès Mondial de Linguistique Africaine Lomé.* Köln: Köppe: 207–221.

MARTEN, LUTZ, 2005. 'The dynamics of agreement and conjunction', *Lingua* 115. 527–547.

MARTEN, LUTZ, 2007. 'Focus strategies and the incremental development of semantic representations: evidence from Bantu', in Enoch Aboh, Katharina Hartmann & Malte Zimmermann (eds.), *Focus strategies: Evidence from African languages.* Berlin: Mouton de Gruyter, 113–135.

MARTEN, LUTZ, 2011. 'Information structure and agreement: Subjects and subject agreement in Swahili and Herero', *Lingua* 121(5). 787–804.

MARTEN, LUTZ. n.d. 'The dynamics of Bantu applied verbs: An analysis at the syntax-pragmatics interface', Ms., SOAS University of London.

MARTEN, LUTZ, & HANNAH GIBSON, 2016. 'Structure building and thematic constraints in Bantu inversion constructions', *Journal of Linguistics* 53(3). 565–607.

MARTEN, LUTZ, RUTH KEMPSON, & MIRIAM BOUZOUITA, 2008. 'Concepts of structural underspecification in Bantu and Romance', in Cécile de Cat & Katherine Demuth (eds.), *The Romance-Bantu connection.* Amsterdam: Benjamins: 3–39.

MARTEN, LUTZ, & NANCY C. KULA, 2011. 'The Prosody of Bemba relative clauses: A case study of the syntax-phonology interface in dynamic syntax', in Ruth Kempson, Christine Howes & Eleni Gregoromichelaki (eds.), *The dynamics of lexical interfaces*, Stanford, CA: CSLI Publications, 61–90.

MARTEN, LUTZ, NANCY C. KULA, & NHLANHLA THWALA, 2007. 'Parameters of morphosyntactic variation in Bantu', *Transactions of the Philological Society* 105(2007). 253–338.

MARTEN, LUTZ, & MAARTEN MOUS, forthcoming. 'Non-valency-changing valency-changing derivations', in Rose-Juliet Anyanwu (ed.), *Transitivity in African languages. Frankfurter Afrikanistische Blätter.*

MARTEN, LUTZ, & MAARTEN MOUS, 2017. 'Valency and expectation in Bantu applicatives', *Linguistics Vanguard* 3(1). 1–15.

MARTEN, LUTZ, & JENNEKE VAN DER WAL, 2015. 'A typology of Bantu inversion Constructions', *Linguistic Variation* 14(2). 318–368.

McCORMACK, ANNA, 2008. *Subject and object pronominal agreement in the Southern Bantu languages: From a dynamic syntax perspective.* Ph.D. dissertation. SOAS, University of London.

MEEUSSEN, ACHILLE EMILLE. 1967. 'Bantu grammatical reconstructions', *Africana Linguistica.* 3(1). 79–121.

MEINHOF, CARL F. M., 1899. *Grundriss einer lautlehre der Bantusprachen.* Leipzig: F. A. Brockhaus.

MIEHE, GUDRUN, 1979. *Die sprache der älteren Swahili-Dichtung: Phonologie und morphologie.* Berlin: Reimer.

MIYAMOTO, EDSON, 2002. 'Case markers as clause boundary inducers in Japanese', *Journal of Psycholinguistic Research* 31(4). 307–347.

NGALAMULUME, BULULE, 1997. Elements de grammaire salampasu (L51): phonologie etmorphologie. *Mémoire de licence.* Lubumbashi: Université nationale du Zaïre.

NURSE, DEREK, 2008. *Tense and aspect in Bantu.* Oxford: Oxford University Press.

NURSE, DEREK, & GERARD PHILIPPSON, 2006. 'Common tense-aspect markers in Bantu', *Journal of African Languages and Linguistics* 27(2). 155–196.

PARTEE, BARBARA H. 1973. 'Some structural analogies between tenses and pronouns in English', *Journal of Philosophy* 70(18). 601–609.

PERRETT, DENISE. 1996. 'A comparison of tense construal in DRT and LDS'. Unpublished paper presented at SOAS, October 1996.

PERRETT, DENISE, 2000. *The dynamic of tense construal in Hadiyya.* Ph.D. dissertation. SOAS University of London.

PICKERING, M., & S. GARROD, 2005. 'Establishing and using routines during dialogue: Implications for psychology and linguistics', in Anne Cutler (ed.), *Twenty-first century psycholinguistics: Four cornerstones.* London: Erlbaum. 85–101.

PRITCHETT, B. L. 1992. *Grammatical competence and parsing performance.* Chicago, IL: University of Chicago Press.

PURVER, MATTHEW, RONNIE CANN, & RUTH KEMPSON, 2006. 'Grammars as parsers: Meeting the dialogue challenge', *Research on Language and Computation* 4 (2–3). 289–326.

REICHENBACH, HANS. 1947. *Elements of symbolic logic.* New York: Harcourt, Collier-Macmillan.

RIEDEL, KRISTINA, 2009. *The syntax of object marking in Sambaa: A comparative Bantu perspective.* Ph.D. dissertation. Leiden University.

SACLEUX, CHARLES P. 1909. *Grammaire des dialectes swahilis.* Paris: Procure des pp. du Saint-Esprit.

SERAKU, TOHRU, 2013a. *Clefts, relatives, and language dynamics: The case of Japanese.* DPhil dissertation, University of Oxford.

SERAKU, TOHRU, 2013b. 'Multiple foci in Japanese clefts revisited: A semantic incrementality account', *Lingua* 137. 145–171.

SERAKU, TOHRU, & HANNAH GIBSON, 2016. 'A dynamic syntax modelling of Japanese and Rangi clefts: Parsing incrementality and the growth of interpretation', *Journal of Language Sciences* 56(2016). 45–67.

SPERBER, DAN & DEIRDRE WILSON, 1995. *Relevance*. Oxford: Blackwell.

SPERBER, DAN & DEIRDRE WILSON. 1997. 'The mapping between the public and the private lexicon' *UCL working papers in linguistics* 9. 107–125.

STEGEN, OLIVER, 2001. 'To be, or not to be: functions of copula and auxiliaries in Rangi'. Unpublished manuscript SIL Tanzania.

STEGEN, OLIVER, 2002. 'Derivational processes in Rangi', *Studies in African Linguistics* 31(1/2). 129–153.

STEGEN, OLIVER, 2011. *In quest of a vernacular writing style for the Rangi of Tanzania: Assumptions, processes, challenges*. Ph.D. dissertation. University of Edinburgh.

WASIKE, AGGREY, 2007. *The left periphery, wh-in-situ and A-bar movement in Lubukusu and other Bantu languages*. Ph.D. dissertation, Cornell University.

WHITELEY, W. H., & J. D. MGANGA. 1969. 'Focus and entailment: Further problems of transitivity in Swahili' *African Language Review* 8(1969). 108–125.

WOOLFORD, ELLEN. 1995. 'Why passive can block object marking', in Akinbiyi Akinlabi (ed.) *Theoretical approaches to African linguistics*. Trenton, NJ: Africa World Press. 199–215.

WOOLFORD, ELLEN, 2001. 'Conditions on object agreement in Ruwund (Bantu)', in Elena Benedicto (ed.) *The Umass volume on indigenous languages*. Amherst, MA: GLSA. 177–201.

WU, YICHENG, 2005. *The dynamic syntax of left and right dislocation*. Ph.D. dissertation. University of Edinburgh.

WU, YICHENG, 2011. 'Towards a dynamic typology of passives', in Ruth Kempson, Christine Howes & Eleni Gregoromichelaki (eds.), *The dynamics of lexical interfaces*, Stanford, CA: CSLI Publications, 131–162.

ZELLER, JOCHEN, 2012. 'Object marking in isiZulu', *Southern African Linguistics and Applied Language Studies* 30(2). 219–235.

ZIERVOGEL, DIRK, & ENOS JOHN MABUZA, 1976. *A grammar of the Swati Language (siSwati)*. Pretoria: J.L van Schaik.

INDEX